MATHS Revision

Dr Chris Farrar

London: The Stationery Office

British Library Cataloguing in Publication Data
A catalogue record for this book is available from the British Library.

ISBN 0 11 702208 X

Printed and bound by Hobbs the Printers Ltd, Totton for The Stationery Office
J0051237 6/98 C50 10170

Published by The Stationery Office and available from:

The Publications Centre
(mail, telephone and fax orders only)
PO Box 276, London SW8 5DT
General enquiries 0171 873 0011
Telephone orders 0171 873 9090
Fax orders 0171 873 8200

The Stationery Office Bookshops
123 Kingsway, London WC2B 6PQ
0171 242 6393   Fax 0171 242 6394
68–69 Bull Street, Birmingham B4 6AD
0121 236 9696   Fax 0121 236 9699
33 Wine Street, Bristol BS1 2BQ
0117 9264306   Fax 0117 9294515
9–21 Princess Street, Manchester M60 8AS
0161 834 7201   Fax 0161 833 0634
16 Arthur Street, Belfast BT1 4GD
01232 238451   Fax 01232 235401
The Stationery Office Oriel Bookshop
The Friary, Cardiff CF1 4AA
01222 395548   Fax 01222 384347
71 Lothian Road, Edinburgh EH3 9AZ

The Stationery Office's Accredited Agents
(see Yellow Pages)

and through good booksellers

Contents

Introduction

At the end of Year 6, almost every child in the United Kingdom between the ages of 10 and 11 will take a national test called 'The National Curriculum Key Stage 2 in Mathematics'.

There are already books that can be bought that test a child using examination-style questions, for example *Key Stage 2 Maths Tests* published by the Stationery Office. However, should a child find difficulty with any question there is no single book that provides the answers and explanation to the questions. Often a parent will want to help but the subject material of school work has changed considerably over the years. Parents may wish to refresh their own knowledge or gain knowledge about the new things that their children are learning about. This book may serve to bridge the gap in parents' knowledge, which would then allow parents to help their own children. The book is also written in a basic style, which should allow children to read and understand the material themselves. The ideal combination is parent and child involvement.

The aim of this book is to provide a parent and child with a thorough account of the syllabus for the National Curriculum Key Stage 2 in mathematics.

There are three main uses of this book:

- as a study aid companion throughout the primary school years between the ages of 7 and 11;
- as a revision guide in preparation before the Key Stage 2 national tests;
- as a guide to answering the questions in the companion book entitled Key Stage 2 Maths Tests published by the Stationery Office.

The National Curriculum for mathematics is divided into four sections:

1. Using and Applying Mathematics
2. Number and Algebra
3. Shape, Space and Measures
4. Handling Data

The tests for 11 year olds only cover sections 2, 3 and 4. The section on Using and Applying Mathematics is only mentioned in this introduction as it is assumed that a child will acquire these skills during the process of learning mathematics. All of the expected techniques are implicitly covered by the contents of this book.

This book covers the syllabus for these examinations very closely.

The section on Number and Algebra deals with the number system, methods of computation and solving numerical problems, relationships between numbers, and basic algebra.

The section on Shape, Space and Measures deals with properties of shape, position and movement, and measures.

The section on Handling Data deals with collecting data, representing data, interpreting data and probability.

The National Curriculum has laid down attainment targets or levels for each subject. It is expected that most children at the age of 11 years attain Levels 3–5.

There are three examinations in Key Stage 2 mathematics of the National Curriculum:

- Test A covers attainment Levels 3–5
- Test B covers attainment Levels 3–5
- Test C covers attainment Level 6.

The first two tests are taken by every child. The third test is taken by some children only. However, this book covers all three tests. The subject material for Level 6 is shaded throughout the book. It is best to cover the unshaded material first. Should a child show an early aptitude for mathematics then the shaded material may be learned and used for the third test.

Many examples have been provided. They are presented as questions with the answers showing how the question is solved. There is at least one example on each topic. More examples are provided for topics that are usually considered more difficult.

There are also many diagrams used to illustrate the principles involved. If the parent and child tackle each topic slowly over a course of time the child should acquire a good knowledge of the subject of mathematics, which will serve them well in the Key Stage 2 examination for mathematics and in the years ahead.

CHAPTER 1

The number system

The number line

The number system consists of:

- positive whole numbers
- negative whole numbers
- positive fractions (part of a positive whole number)
- negative fractions (part of a negative whole number)

The number line is a convenient way of representing these different types of numbers on one line.

QUESTION: Draw a line from each of the following numbers to show where it would go on the number line.

254   101   990   1600   1400

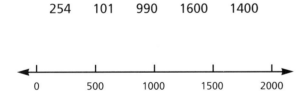

ANSWER:

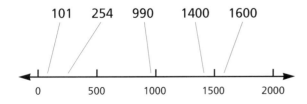

Whole numbers

A number is composed of digits. A digit is a numeral between 0 and 9. Each digit within a number has a special significance. The place of the digit determines how large or small a number is.

Each digit of a number may represent a:

- unit (U)
- ten (T)
- hundred (H)
- thousand (Th.)
- ten thousand (TTh.), etc.

depending on where the digit is placed.

The place of a digit represents its value:

- ten units make one ten, 10
- ten tens make one hundred, 100
- ten hundreds make one thousand, 1000
- ten thousands make one ten thousand, 10000

A simple counting frame can be used to show the place value of digits. In the example, each digit within the number represents a unit, ten, hundred or thousand.

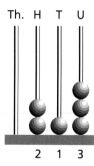
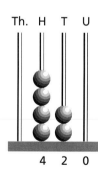
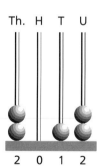

The frame on the left:
represents the number two hundred and thirteen, written as 213.

The middle frame:
represents the number four hundred and twenty, written as 420.

The frame on the right:
represents the number two thousand and twelve, written as 2012.

The table shows some different numbers and how they are represented and written.

The number system is based on the number ten, so 10, 100 and 1000 are important numbers.

Number	Th.	H	T	U	Written
Seven	0	0	0	7	7
Ten	**0**	**0**	**1**	**0**	**10**
Ninety-nine	0	0	9	9	99
One hundred	**0**	**1**	**0**	**0**	**100**
One hundred and seven	0	1	0	7	107
One hundred and ten	0	1	1	0	110
Nine hundred and ninety-nine	0	9	9	9	999
One thousand	**1**	**0**	**0**	**0**	**1000**
One thousand and seven	1	0	0	7	1007
Nine thousand nine hundred and ninety-nine	9	9	9	9	9999

Equals

If two numbers are the same then they are said to be equal.
The = sign is used as a symbol to represent 'equal to'.

Example: The number 14563 can be written as

$14563 = 10000 + 4000 + 500 + 60 + 3$

QUESTION:

Write the following numbers in the same way as the example.

28058, 67526, 498527

ANSWER:

$28058 = 20000 + 8000 + 50 + 8$

$67526 = 60000 + 7000 + 500 + 20 + 6$

$498527 = 400000 + 90000 + 8000 + 500 + 20 + 7$

Greater than

A number with two digits will always be greater than a number with one digit. A number with three digits will always be greater than a number with two digits, and so on.

For example, 10 is greater than 7; 23 is greater than 9; 100 is greater than 99. In order to decide how large a number is it is important to look at the left-most number and the number of digits.

The > sign is used to represent 'greater than'. For example, 23 > 9.

QUESTION: Write these numbers in ascending order (lowest first).

100 801 99 70 1001 999

ANSWER:

70 99 100 801 999 1001

Less than

The < sign is used to represent 'less than'. For example, 9 < 23.

QUESTION: Decide whether the following numbers are equal to, greater than or less than the number 12.

3 10 12 15 18 100

ANSWER:

3 < 12   10 < 12   12 = 12   15 > 12   18 > 12   100 > 12

QUESTION: Join each number to its correct description.

| Between five thousand and ten thousand | Between a thousand and five thousand | Less than fifty | Greater than twenty thousand |

40001   40   8000   4001

ANSWER:

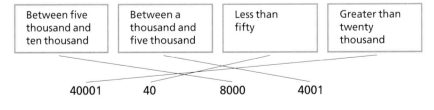

40001   40   8000   4001

Working with 10s, 100s and 1000s

Our number system uses the 'decimal' system. The word 'Dec' means 'ten'. So our number system is based on the number 10.

Rounding is a way of approximating numbers. It is important to be able to round a number to the nearest 10 or 100.

Approximating numbers to the nearest 10

In order to round a number to the nearest ten, follow the rules below.

Examine the 'units' column:

- If the number is greater than or equal to 5, then round up to the next ten: increase the tens column by one.
- If the number is less than 5, then round down to the ten: do not change the tens column.

For example, the table describes how some numbers are rounded up or down to the nearest 10.

Number	Reasoning	Number to the nearest 10
27	7 is greater than 5 so round up	30
44	4 is less than 5 so round down	40
65	5 is equal to 5 so round up	70
81	1 is less than 5 so round down	80
98	8 is greater than 5 so round up	100

QUESTION: Approximate 46 + 33 to the nearest 10.

ANSWER:

As 6 is greater than 5, round up 46 to 50.

As 3 is less than 5, round down 33 to 30.

So 46 + 33 rounds to 50 + 30 = 80.

Approximating numbers to the nearest 100

In order to round a number to the nearest hundred, follow the rules below.

Examine the 'tens' column:

- If the number is greater than or equal to 50, then round up to the next hundred: increase the hundreds column by one.
- If the number is less than 50, then round down to the hundred: do not change the hundreds column.

Number	Reasoning	Number to the nearest 100
173	73 is greater than 50 so round up	200
450	50 is equal to 50 so round up	500
543	43 is less then 50 so round down	500
749	49 is less than 50 so round down	700
999	99 is greater than 50 so round up	1000

QUESTION: Approximate 236 + 790 to the nearest 100.

ANSWER:

As 36 is less than 50 round down 236 to 200.

As 90 is greater than 50 round up 790 to 800.

So 236 + 790 rounds to 200 + 800 = 1000.

Multiplying by 10 or 100

Whenever a whole number is multiplied by 10, add a zero at the end of the number. For example:

Number	×**10**
6	6**0**
10	10**0**
120	120**0**
5025	5025**0**

Similarly, whenever a number is multiplied by 100 add two zeros at the end of the number. For example:

Number	×**100**
6	6**00**
10	10**00**
120	120**00**
5025	5025**00**

Dividing by 10 or 100

Whenever a whole number is divided by 10, subtract a zero from the number. For example:

Number	÷10
60	6
100	10
1200	120
50250	5025

Similarly, whenever a whole number is divided by 100, subtract two zeros from the number. For example:

Number	÷100
600	6
1000	10
12000	120
502500	5025

Using the above rules, we are able to calculate multiplication and division of some large numbers with zeros on the end of them very quickly. For example:

Multiply		Total of zeros	Result
60 × 40	6 × 4 = 24	2	24**00**
400 × 30	4 × 3 = 12	3	12**000**
200 × 500	2 × 5 = 10	4	10**0000**

Divide		Difference of zeros	Result
600 ÷ 20	6 ÷ 2 = 3	1	3**0**
800 ÷ 4	8 ÷ 4 = 2	2	2**00**
900000 ÷ 300	9 ÷ 3 = 3	3	3**000**

Negative numbers

Negative numbers occur in everyday situations. For example, when the temperature drops three degrees below 0°C then the temperature is written as –3°C. The difference in temperature between 2°C and –3°C is 5°.

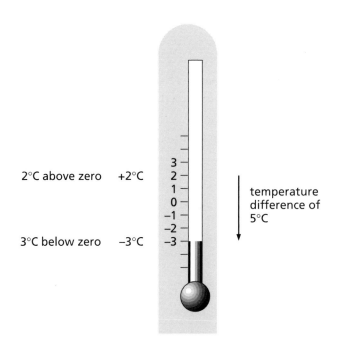

2°C above zero   +2°C

temperature difference of 5°C

3°C below zero   –3°C

If a person spends more money than he or she has in their bank account, then the total of their money is below zero. For example, if a person has £20 in the bank and he or she spends £30, that person will have –£10 in their account.

QUESTION:

Arrange the following numbers in order, starting with the smallest.
7   –2   –10   18   –1   3   0

ANSWER:

–10   –2   –1   0   3   7   18

Parts of a whole number

Parts of a whole number are called fractions. The following are different ways of representing fractions:

- decimals
- fractions
- percentages

Decimals

It is possible to represent a fraction as a decimal. Decimals are based on the number 10. The set of digits before the decimal point is called the whole number, and the set of digits after the decimal point is called the fraction. The decimal point separates the whole number from the fraction.

$$4.56$$

Whole number ⌐ ⌐ Fraction

Decimal point

Decimals are most commonly used in measurements and money.

Measurements and money

Although measurements and money are usually expressed as decimals, they are referred to differently. For example:

Value	Spoken as
£4.56	Four pounds fifty-six
4.56 m	Four point five six metres

QUESTION: John is 155 cm tall. Express this as a decimal in metres.

ANSWER: 155 cm = 1.55 m (one point five five metres)

QUESTION: Add up the total cost for the following shopping bill.

Item	Price £
Bread	0.80
1 pint milk	1.20
Lemonade	0.75
$\frac{1}{4}$ lb ham	1.80
$\frac{1}{2}$ kg apples	2.30

ANSWER: The total shopping bill adds up to £6.85

Fractions

Another way of representing parts of a whole number is to use fractions. There are many examples of fractions in everyday life. Fractions are used to describe parts of a unit of time, such as an hour, or parts of a quantity. The table illustrates some common uses of fractions.

Time	$\frac{1}{2}$ hour lunch break
	$\frac{1}{4}$ hour playtime
	$6\frac{1}{2}$ hours in a school day
Measurements	$\frac{1}{2}$ pint of milk
	$\frac{1}{2}$ kg cheese
	$3\frac{1}{2}$ miles to the town centre

Some common fractions are shown in the table.

Fraction	Name
$\frac{1}{10}$	One-tenth
$\frac{1}{4}$	A quarter
$\frac{1}{2}$	A half
$\frac{1}{3}$	One-third
$\frac{3}{4}$	Three-quarters
1	A whole

The diagrams show how fractions can be shown.

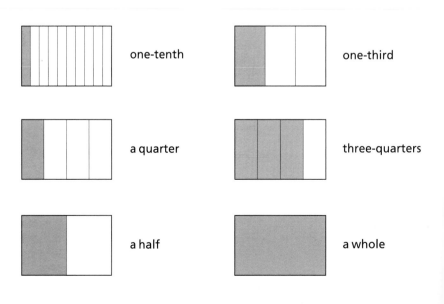

one-tenth

one-third

a quarter

three-quarters

a half

a whole

QUESTION:
Using the square grid below, shade the following fractions.

$\frac{1}{4}$ $\frac{1}{2}$ $\frac{3}{4}$ 1

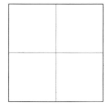

ANSWER:

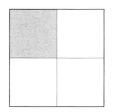 $\frac{1}{4}$ shaded

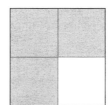 $\frac{3}{4}$ shaded

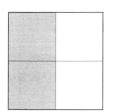 $\frac{1}{2}$ shaded

   Whole one shaded

QUESTION:
Shade in half of these squares

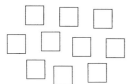

ANSWER:

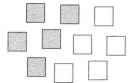

QUESTION:
Shade in a quarter of these squares

ANSWER:

QUESTION:

Shade in three-quarters of each set of circles.

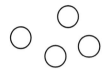
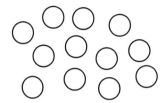

ANSWER:

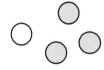
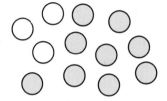

QUESTION:

What fraction of the tiled floors is shaded?

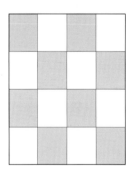
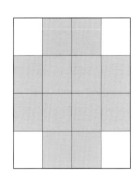
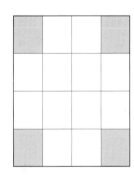

ANSWER:

$\frac{8}{16} = \frac{1}{2}$ $\frac{12}{16} = \frac{3}{4}$ $\frac{4}{16} = \frac{1}{4}$

Percentages

Another way of representing parts of a whole is to use percentages. Percentages represent numbers as a fraction of 100. The symbol used to represent 'per cent' is %.

'Per' means 'divide by'. 'Cent' means '100'.
So 'per cent' means 'divide by 100'.

For example:
- 50% can be represented as $\frac{50}{100}$
- 25% can be represented as $\frac{25}{100}$
- 75% can be represented as $\frac{75}{100}$

Example: If a child has scored 60 marks out of 100 marks in a maths test then the child has scored 60%.

The table shows how each test score may be represented as a percentage.

Score	Percentage
$\frac{45}{100}$	45%
$\frac{63}{100}$	63%
$\frac{74}{100}$	74%
$\frac{92}{100}$	92%
$\frac{4}{10}$	40%
$\frac{3}{10}$	30%
$\frac{8}{10}$	80%
$\frac{7}{10}$	70%
$\frac{26}{50}$	52%
$\frac{31}{50}$	62%
$\frac{45}{50}$	90%
$\frac{18}{50}$	36%

Equivalent fractions

Three different ways of representing parts of a whole number have been shown. This table shows the equivalent decimals and percentages for some common fractions.

Fraction	Decimal	Percentage
$\frac{1}{4}$	0.25	25%
$\frac{1}{2}$	0.50	50%
$\frac{3}{4}$	0.75	75%
1	1.00	100%

Methods of computation and solving numerical problems

The four basic arithmetic operations

This chapter examines ways of combining whole numbers and parts of whole numbers by using one of the four basic arithmetic operations:

- addition
- subtraction
- multiplication
- division

Addition

Addition is another name for 'sum' or 'total'. The symbol + is used to represent 'add'. We can use a calculator to perform addition very quickly, but it is good to be able to perform addition without the use of a calculator.

QUESTION: Find the missing number. ? + 7 = 20

ANSWER: 13

QUESTION: Find the missing number. 23 + 46 = ?

ANSWER: 69

QUESTION: Find the missing number. 87 + 76 = ?

ANSWER: The last addition may be too difficult to do in your head. Write the sum down as shown. Each unit, ten, hundred and thousand must line up underneath each other.

H	T	U
	8	7
+	7₁	6
1	6	3

In words:

- The units column shows 7 + 6 = 13U. Carry 10U as 1T to the T column. Write 3 as the total for the U column.
- In the tens column, 8 + 7 = 15T. 15 + 1T carried = 16T. Carry 10T as 1H to the H column. Write 6 as the total for the T column.
- In the hundreds column, there is only the 1H carried. Write 1 as the total for the H column.

QUESTION: Add up the following.

Th.	H	T	U
	4	5	6
+	7	4	5

ANSWER:

Th.	H	T	U
	4	5	6
+	7₁	4₁	5
1	2	0	1

In words:

- In the units column, 6 + 5 = 11U. Carry 10U as 1T to the T column. Write 1 as the total for the U column.
- In the tens column, 5 + 4 = 9T. 9 + 1T carried = 10T . Carry 10T as 1H to the H column. Write 0 as the total for the T column.
- In the hundreds column, 4 + 7 =11H. 11 + 1H carried = 12H. Carry 10H as 1Th. to the Th. column. Write 2 as the total for the H column.
- In the thousands column, there is only the 1Th. carried. Write 1 as the total for the Th. column.

Subtraction

Subtraction is another word for 'take away', 'difference' or 'minus'. The symbol – is used to represent 'subtract'. We can use a calculator to perform subtraction very quickly, but it is good to be able to perform subtraction without the use of a calculator.

QUESTION: Find the missing number. $? - 7 = 12$

ANSWER: 19

QUESTION: Find the missing number.   64 − 31 = ?

ANSWER: 33

QUESTION: Find the missing number.   81 − 36 = ?

ANSWER: As the numbers in the last question are larger, it is easier to write the subtraction down.

T	U
8̸7	₁1
− 3	6
4	**5**

In words:

- In the units column, 1 − 6. This cannot be done, so change one T in the T column into 10U. This gives us 11U in the U column, and the 8T in the T column becomes 7T. 11 − 6 = 5U. Write 5 as the total in the U column.

- In the tens column, 7 − 3 = 4T. Write 4 as the total for the T column.

QUESTION: Subtract the following.

H	T	U
8	6	7
− 5	3	5

ANSWER:

H	T	U
8	6	7
− 5	3	5
3	**3**	**2**

In words:

- In the units column, 7 − 5 = 2U. Write 2 as the total for the U column.

- In the tens column, 6 − 3 = 3T. Write 3 as the total for the T column.

- In the hundreds column, 8 − 5 = 3H. Write 3 as the total for the H column.

QUESTION: Subtract the following.

H	T	U
8	5	2
− 4	7	5

ANSWER:

H	T	U
8̸7	5̸₁4	₁2
− 4	7	5
3	**7**	**7**

In words:

- In the units column, 2 – 5. This cannot be done, so change one T in the T column into 10U. 2U becomes 12U in the U column, and 5T becomes 4T in the T column. 12 – 5 = 7U. Write 7 as the total for the U column.

- In the tens column, 4 – 7. This cannot be done, so change one H in the H column into 10T. 4T becomes 14T, and 8H becomes 7H. 14 – 7 = 7T. Write 7 as the total for the T column.

- In the hundreds column, 7 – 4 = 3H. Write 3 as the total for the H column.

Multiplication

Multiplication is repeated addition. For example, writing $6 \times 2 = 12$ is a short way of calculating $2 + 2 + 2 + 2 + 2 + 2$. It is important to learn the multiplication tables up to ten. For larger numbers, long multiplication and a calculator are usually needed.

×	1	2	3	4	5	6	7	8	9	10
1	1	2	3	4	5	6	7	8	9	10
2	2	4	6	8	10	12	14	16	18	20
3	3	6	9	12	15	18	21	24	27	30
4	4	8	12	16	20	24	28	32	36	40
5	5	10	15	20	25	30	35	40	45	50
6	6	12	18	24	30	36	42	48	54	60
7	7	14	21	28	35	42	49	56	63	70
8	8	16	24	32	40	48	56	64	72	80
9	9	18	27	36	45	54	63	72	81	90
10	10	20	30	40	50	60	70	80	90	100

Multiplication table up to 10

This table should be learned.

Long multiplication

Long multiplication is used when the numbers are too large to work out in your head.

QUESTION: Work out the following.

T	U
2	9
×	5

ANSWER:

H	T	U
	2₄	9
	×	5
1	**4**	**5**

In words:

- In the units column, 5 × 9 = 45U. Carry 40U as 4T to the T column. Write 5 as the total for the U column.

- In the tens column, 5 × 2 = 10T. 10 + 4T carried = 14. Carry 10T as 1H to the H column. Write 4 as the total for the T column.

- In the hundreds column, there is only the 1H carried. Write 1 as the total for the H column.

QUESTION: Work out the following.

Th.	H	T	U
		4	7
	×	3	5

ANSWER:

Th.	H	T	U
		4₃,₂	7
	×	3	5
	2	3	5
1	4	1	0
1	**6**	**4**	**5**

In words:

- In the units column
  5 × 7 = 35U. Carry 30U as 3T into the T column.
  Write 5 in the U column of the first row of totals.

  5 × 4 = 20T. 20 + 3T carried = 23T. Carry 2T into the H column. Write 3 in the T column and 2 in the H column in the first row of totals.

- In the tens column
  Write 0 under the U column in the second row of totals.

  $3 \times 7 = 21T$. Carry the 2T into the H column.
  Write 1 in the T column of the second row of totals.

  $3 \times 4 = 12H$. $12 + 2H$ carried $= 14H$. Carry 10H into the Th. column.
  Write 4 in the H column and 1 in the Th. column in the second row
  of totals.

- Adding the rows
  $5 + 0 = 5U$. Write 5 in the U column of the final total. $3 + 1 = 4T$.
  Write 4 in the T column of the final total.

  $2 + 4 = 6H$. Write 6 in the H column of the final total. $0 + 1 = 1Th$.
  Write 1 in the Th. column of the final total.

QUESTION: Work out the following.

TTh.	Th.	H	T	U
		6	4	7
		×	5	2

ANSWER:

TTh.	Th.	H	T	U
		6 $_2$	4 $_{1,3}$	7
		×	5	2
	1	2	9	4
3	2	3 $_1$	5	0
3	**3**	**6**	**4**	**4**

In words:

- In the units column
  $2 \times 7 = 14U$. Carry 10U as 1T into the T column.
  Write 4 in the U column of the first row of totals.

  $2 \times 4 = 8T$. $8 + 1T$ carried $= 9T$.
  Write 9 in the T column of the first row of totals.

  $2 \times 6 = 12H$. Carry 10H as 1Th. into the Th. column.
  Write 2 as the total for the H column and 1 as the total for the
  Th. column in the first row of totals.

- In the tens column
  Write 0 in the U column in the second row of totals.

  $5 \times 7 = 35T$. Carry 30T as 3H into the H column.
  Write 5 in the T column of the second row of totals.

  $5 \times 4 = 20H$. $20 + 3H$ carried $= 23H$. Carry 20H as 2Th. into the Th.
  column. Write 3 as the total for the H column in the second row of
  totals.

  $5 \times 6 = 30Th$. $30 + 2Th$. carried $= 32$. Carry 30Th. as 3 TTh. into the
  TTh. column. Write 2 as the total for the Th. column and 3 as the
  total for the TTh. column in the second row of totals.

- Adding the rows

  4 + 0 = 4U. Write 4 as the final total for the U column.

  9 + 5 = 14. Carry 10T into the H column.
  Write 4 as the total for the T column.

  2 + 3 = 5H. 5 + 1H carried = 6H.
  Write 6 as the total for the H column.

  1 + 2 = 3Th. Write 3 as the total for the Th. column.

  0 + 3 = 3Thh. Write 3 as the total for the TTh. column.

Division

Division is repeated subtraction or sharing. The symbol used for division is ÷.

If 8 sweets are divided between 2 friends, each friend will receive 4 sweets. This is written mathematically as 8 ÷ 2 = 4. This means that it is possible to take 2 away from 8 four times, and that 8 shared between 2 gives four each.

Division is the opposite, or inverse operation, of multiplication. Knowing your multiplication tables up to ten makes divisions easier to work out.

QUESTION: Work out 63 ÷ 7.

ANSWER: Because we know that 9 × 7 = 63, then it is possible to work backwards.
63 ÷ 7 = 9.

QUESTION: Work out 63 ÷ 9.

ANSWER: Because we know that 9 × 7 = 63, then it is possible to work backwards.
63 ÷ 9 = 7.

Remainder

It is not always possible to divide a number by another number exactly. If this happens there is a remainder.

QUESTION: 12 sweets are to be divided between 5 children. How many sweets are left over?

ANSWER: 12 ÷ 5 = 2 remainder 2. So there will be 2 sweets left over.

QUESTION: Divide 92 by 10.

ANSWER: $92 \div 10 = 9$ remainder 2.

QUESTION: Which of the following numbers have no remainder after division by 2?
11, 4, 20, 10, 13, 29

ANSWER: 2 divides into 4, 20, 10 exactly. 11, 13 and 29 have remainders.

QUESTION: Which of the following numbers have no remainder after division by 5?
42, 55, 60, 74, 82

ANSWER: 5 divides into 55 and 60 exactly. 42, 74 and 82 have remainders.

Long division

When the numbers involved in a division are large, you have to use long division or a calculator. In long division you continue to divide until there are no more remainders. The examples below show the technique for long division.

Example: Divide 156 by 12.

```
            1   3
        ┌──────────
1   2   │ 1   5   6
          1   2
          ─────
              3   6
              3   6
              ─────
                  0
```

In words:

- 12 into 1 will not divide.
- 12 into 15 will divide once with a remainder of 3. Write 1 above the tens.
- $1 \times 12 = 12$. $15 - 12 = 3$. Move the digit 6 down to the remainder of 3 to give 36.
- 12 into 36 divides 3 times. Write 3 above the units.
- $3 \times 12 = 36$. $36 - 36 = 0$. No remainder.
- 12 divides into 156 13 times.

It is possible to check the answer by multiplying 13 by 12. $13 \times 12 = 156$.

Example: Divide 874 by 46.

```
                1   9
    4   6 | 8   7   4
            4   6
          ─────────
            4   1   4
            4   1   4
          ─────────
                    0
```

In words:

- 46 into 8 will not divide.
- 46 into 87 will divide once with a remainder of 41. Write 1 above the tens.
- $1 \times 46 = 46$. $87 - 46 = 41$. Move the digit 4 down to the remainder of 41 to give 414.
- 46 into 414 divides 9 times. Write 9 above the units.
- $9 \times 46 = 414$. $414 - 414 = 0$. No remainder.
- 46 divides into 874 19 times.

It is possible to check the answer by multiplying 19 by 46.
$19 \times 46 = 874$.

Mental arithmetic

It is not always possible to write down every mathematical problem that we have to work out, and we may not have a calculator when we need to work something out. For example, when you are paying for things or deciding what you can afford to buy in a shop you have to work out the arithmetic in your head. This can involve addition, subtraction, multiplication and division.

QUESTION: How much money is in the set of coins below?

ANSWER: £1.58

QUESTION: How much money is in the set of coins below?

ANSWER: £3.84

QUESTION: Apples cost 20p each. How much would 8 apples cost?

ANSWER: 8 × 20p = £1.60

QUESTION: 4 lemons cost 60p. What would one lemon cost?

ANSWER: 60 ÷ 4 = 15p

QUESTION: Andrew wishes to buy some sweets. He has a £1 coin, one 50p coin, and two 20p coins. He buys sweets costing 95p. What coin or coins should he give the shopkeeper? Does he receive any change? If he receives any change, what is it?

ANSWER: Adding up the small coins, the coins amount to 50p + 20p + 20p = 90p. This would not be enough, so Andrew has to give the shopkeeper the £1 coin. There are 100p in one £1, so after spending 95p he will receive 5p change.

QUESTION: Mr Ceesay wants to park his car in a car park for two hours at a charge of £1.85. He has the following coins in his pocket: three 50p coins, two 20p coins, three 10p coins and four 5p coins. What coins should Mr Ceesay put into the meter?

ANSWER: Three 50p coins, one 20p coin, one 10p coin and one 5p coin.

QUESTION: Nimish has a £1 coin, two 50p coins, one 20p coin and three 10p coins. How much money does he have altogether?

ANSWER: Try to add the coins to make £s and 50s. For example, the two 50p coins make one £. The one 20p and three 10p make 50p. So Nimish has £2.50.

QUESTION: Sian goes to a shop with £12.00. She spends £6.40 on clothes and £2.50 on toys. How much money does she go home with?

ANSWER: £6.40 + £2.50 = £8.90. Subtract this from £12.00 to give £3.10. Sian goes home with £3.10.

When you have to work out an addition, look for numbers that add up to 10. This helps you to add up more quickly.

QUESTION: Add the following numbers together. 23, 48, 52, 67

ANSWER: Look for numbers that add up 10.
8 and 2 make 10, and 3 and 7 make 10.

$$
\begin{array}{r}
2\ \ 3 \\
4\ \ 8 \\
5\ \ 2 \\
+\ \ 6_2\ \ 7 \\
\hline
1\ \ 9\ \ 0 \\
\hline
\end{array}
$$

Arithmetic problems

If you can work out arithmetic calculations, you can work out everyday types of problems.

QUESTION: A man pays £550 a month to his building society as repayments on a loan to buy a house. How much does he pay back in one year?

ANSWER: 12 × £550 = £6,600

QUESTION: The school bus travels 24 miles each day. How many miles will the bus travel in one school week of 5 days?

ANSWER: 5 × 24 = 120 miles.

QUESTION: A car travels 40 miles on a gallon of petrol. How far will it travel on nine gallons of petrol?

ANSWER: 9 × 40 = 360 miles

QUESTION: You can fit eight sweets into a box at a time. How many sweet boxes are needed for 24 sweets? How many sweet boxes are needed for 30 sweets? How many sweets are there in the partially filled box?

ANSWER:
24 ÷ 8 = 3, so 3 boxes are needed for 24 sweets.
30 ÷ 8 = 3 remainder 6, so 4 boxes are needed and there are 6 sweets in the partially filled box.

QUESTION: A ticket for a pop concert costs £10.50. How many tickets can be bought for £100? What would 7 tickets cost?

ANSWER:
Divide £100 by £10.50 to work out the number of tickets.
100 ÷ 10.50 = 9 remainder £5.50, so 9 tickets can be bought.
7 tickets would cost 7 × £10.50 = £73.50

QUESTION: A car travels 42 miles on 1 gallon of petrol. How many gallons are needed to travel 378 miles?

ANSWER: 378 ÷ 42 = 9, so 9 gallons will be needed.

QUESTION: 48 felt tip pens cost £2.88. How much would 1 pen cost? How much would 12 pens cost?

ANSWER:
1 pen costs 288 ÷ 48 = 6p
12 pens would cost 12 × 6 = 72p

QUESTION: 20 identical textbooks measure 30 cm wide. What is the width of 7 textbooks?

ANSWER: Work out the width of one book first.
20 books are 30 cm wide
1 book is 30 ÷ 20 cm = 1.5 cm wide
7 books are 7 × 1.5 = 10.5 cm wide

Calculations with negative numbers

Any number less than zero is a negative number. You will often come across negative numbers in everyday life. You can work out simple calculations with negative numbers.

When working out sums with negative numbers, the following rules apply:

- Two minuses make a plus.
- A plus and a minus make a minus.

QUESTION: What is the temperature difference between +2°C and –3°C?

ANSWER: The difference between 2 and –3 is 5. This can be written as:

$2 - (-3) = 2 + 3 = 5$

QUESTION: What is the temperature difference between –3°C and –2°C?

ANSWER: $-3 - (-2) = -3 + 2 = -1$

QUESTIONS: Work out the following.

a) $5 - 7 = ?$
b) $-3 + (-5) = ?$
c) $-7 - (-6) = ?$
d) $-10 + (-8) = ?$

ANSWERS:

a) $5 - 7 = -2$
b) $-3 + (-5) = -3-5 = -8$
c) $-7 - (-6) = -7 + 6 = -1$
d) $-10 + (-8) = -10 - 8 = -18$

QUESTIONS: Find the missing numbers.

a) $? + 3 = -6$
b) $-8 + ? = -17$
c) $-7 - ? = 12$

ANSWERS:

a) $-9 + 3 = -6$. Answer –9
b) $-8 + (-9) = -17$. Answer = –9
c) $-7 - (-19) = -7 + 19 = 12$. Answer = –19

City	Temperature
London	7°C
New York	−5°C
Moscow	−10°C
Toronto	−20°C

QUESTIONS: Using the table, work out the following.

a) What is the difference in temperature between London and New York?

b) What is the difference in temperature between Moscow and Toronto?

c) What is the difference in temperature between London and Toronto?

d) What is the difference in temperature between Moscow and London?

ANSWERS:

a) $7 - (-5) = 7 + 5 = 12$. London is 12°C warmer than New York.

b) $-10 - (-20) = -10 + 20 = 10$. Moscow is 10°C warmer than Toronto.

c) $7 - (-20) = 27$. London is 27°C warmer than Toronto.

d) $-10 - (7) = -17$. Moscow is 17°C colder than London.

Calculations with decimals

When you are buying things, or measuring things, you often have to work out calculations with decimals.

QUESTION: In a supermarket, oranges are for sale at 15p each. Bananas are for sale at 50p a pair. How much would 5 oranges and 6 bananas cost? Give your answer in pounds and pence.

ANSWER:
5 oranges cost $5 \times 15 = 75$p
6 bananas cost $3 \times 50 = 150$p
Total cost = £0.75 + £1.50 = £2.25

QUESTION: A piece of wood, 14 m long, is cut into four smaller pieces, of lengths 3.40 m, 4.02 m, 2.56 m and 1.95 m. What is the length of the remaining long piece of wood?

ANSWER: Add up the lengths of the smaller pieces of wood and take this result away from the original length to find the remaining piece of wood.

Total of smaller pieces:

```
  3 .  4  0
  4 .  0  2
  2 .  5  6
 ₁1 .  9₁ 5
 ─────────────
 11 .  9  3
```

Take this sum from the original 14.00 m.
14.00 − 11.93 = 2.07 m

QUESTION: A mother buys three books for her children costing £5.00, £7.50, and £9.45. How much change will the mother receive after paying for the books with a £50 note?

ANSWER: Work out the total price for all the books. Take this result away from £50 to find the change.

```
  5 .  0  0
  7 .  5  0
  9 .  4  5
 ─────────────
 21 .  9  5
```

£50 − £21.95 = £28.05

Calculations with fractions

Whenever we write a fraction we write two numbers. The top number is called the numerator and the bottom number is called the denominator.

$$\text{Numerator} \longrightarrow \frac{1}{2} \longleftarrow \text{Denominator}$$

Simplifying fractions

If a number can divide into the numerator and denominator it is called a common factor. If there is a common factor, the fraction can be made simpler. For example, $\frac{5}{10}$ can be written in a simpler way. 5 is a common factor because it will divide into the top and bottom numbers of the fraction:

5 'goes into' 5 once $\frac{5^{\ 1}}{10^{\ 2}}$

5 'goes into' 10 twice

So $\frac{5}{10} = \frac{1}{2}$

QUESTION: Simplify the following fractions.

$\frac{3}{6}, \ \frac{4}{8}, \ \frac{10}{15}, \ \frac{15}{20}, \ \frac{12}{16}, \ \frac{3}{9}$

ANSWER:

3 divides into 3 once and 3 divides into 6 twice so

$\frac{3^{\ 1}}{6^{\ 2}} = \frac{1}{2}$

4 divides into 4 once and 4 divides into 8 twice so

$\frac{4^{\ 1}}{8^{\ 2}} = \frac{1}{2}$

5 divides into 10 twice and 5 divides into 15 three times so

$\frac{10^{\ 2}}{15^{\ 3}} = \frac{2}{3}$

5 divides into 15 three times and 5 divides into 20 four times so

$\frac{15^{\ 3}}{20^{\ 4}} = \frac{3}{4}$

4 divides into 12 three times and 4 divides into 16 four times so

$\frac{12^{\ 3}}{16^{\ 4}} = \frac{3}{4}$

3 divides into 3 once and 3 divides into 9 three times so

$\frac{3^{\ 1}}{9^{\ 2}} = \frac{1}{2}$

Calculations with percentages

You can work out percentages by using a calculator.

QUESTION: Find 60% of 200.
Press:

ANSWER:

QUESTION: What is 10% of £14?
Press:

ANSWER:

QUESTION: What is 40% of 500g?
Press:

ANSWER:

Rounding, estimation and approximations

Rounding

Numbers can be rounded to the nearest 10 and 100.

QUESTION: Write these numbers to the nearest 10.
37, 62, 96

ANSWER:
As 7 is greater than 5, round up to the next ten. 37 becomes 40.
As 2 is less than 5, round down to the ten. 62 becomes 60.
As 6 is greater than 5, round up to the next 10. 96 becomes 100.

Estimation

It can be helpful to estimate the answer to a sum, so that you can come up with an answer more quickly.

QUESTION: Estimate the following to the nearest 100.
615 + 580 + 99

ANSWER:
An estimate is 600 + 600 + 100 = 1300.
The accurate answer is 615 + 580 + 99 = 1294.

QUESTION: What is the cost of 19 ice creams at 31p each?

ANSWER:
An estimate is 20 ice creams at 30p = £6.00
The accurate answer is 19 ice creams at 31p = £5.89

QUESTION: Postcards cost 27p each and stamps cost 29p each.
If Mrs McDonald bought 8 postcards and 8 stamps, approximately how much money did she spend?

ANSWER:
An estimate is:
8 postcards at 25p = £2.00
8 stamps at 30p each = £2.40
Total = £4.40

The accurate answer is:
8 postcards at 27p = £2.16
8 stamps at 29p each = £2.32
Total = £4.48

Ratios

When two or more substances are mixed together it is often important to know how much of each substance there is in the mixture. For example when cooking, many recipes say 'add 4 parts water to 1 part stock'. This means that for every unit of stock added there should be 4 units of water. Ratios are used in chemistry and in everyday jobs such as finance.

The : symbol is used for ratios. Ratios are expressed in the form $m:n$ where m and n are numbers. Often one of the numbers is 1.

QUESTION: The ratio of Euan's age to his father is 1:3. Euan is 13 years old. How old is his father?

ANSWER: Euan's father is 3 times the age of his son, so Euan's father is $3 \times 13 = 39$ years.

QUESTION: £21 is to be shared between John and Susan at a ratio of 2:5. How much do they each receive?

ANSWER: $2 + 5 = 7$.
So the money is shared in amounts of sevenths.

John receives $\frac{2}{7}$ of 21 = £6.

Susan receives $\frac{5}{7}$ of 21 = £15.

QUESTION: Sima is going to share 60 sweets between her friends using the ratio of their ages, 9:10:11. How many sweets does each friend receive?

ANSWER: $9 + 10 + 11 = 30$, so the sweets will be shared in units of thirtieths.

The first friend receives $\frac{9}{30}$ of 60 = 18 sweets

The second friend receives $\frac{10}{30}$ of 60 = 20 sweets

The third friend receives $\frac{11}{30}$ of 60 = 22 sweets

CHAPTER 3

Relationships between numbers

Number sequences

A number sequence is a set of numbers with a rule that links one number with the next.

Counting in different sizes of step

In the simplest type of number sequences, the same number is added to each number of the sequence to give the next number.

QUESTION: Write down the next two numbers in the following sequence. 2, 3, 4, 5, 6, __ , __

ANSWER: The numbers are increasing in steps of one. Add 1 to each number of the sequence to get the next number in the sequence.
2, 3, 4, 5, 6, **7, 8**

QUESTION: Write down the next two numbers in the following sequence. 5, 10, 15, 20, __ , __

ANSWER: The numbers are increasing in steps of five. Add 5 to each number of the sequence to get the next number in the sequence.
5, 10, 15, 20, **25, 30**

QUESTION: Write down the next two numbers in the following sequence. 11, 21, 31, 41, __ , __

ANSWER: The numbers are increasing in steps of ten. Add 10 to each number of the sequence to get the next number in the sequence.
11, 21, 31, 41, **51, 61**

QUESTION: Write down the next number in the following sequence.
1, 3, 6, 10, 15, __

ANSWER: The size of the step between one number and the next increases by one each time. 1 + **2** = 3, 3 + **3** = 6, 6 + **4** = 10, 10 + **5** = 15. The new numbers are increased by 2, 3, 4, 5, and so on, so the next time the number will increase by 6. 15 + 6 = 21.
1, 3, 6, 10, 15, **21**

Odd and even numbers

An even number is a number that can be divided by 2 without a remainder. An odd number is a number that cannot be divided exactly by 2. Odd and even numbers often appear in sequences of numbers.

A way of working out whether a number is odd or even is to look at the last digit. If the last digit is 0, 2, 4, 6, or 8 then the number will be even. If the last digit is 1, 3, 5, 7 or 9 then the number is odd.

QUESTION: Which of the following numbers are even and which are odd? 42 80 19 93 15

ANSWER: 42 and 80 are even because they can be divided by 2 exactly. The last digit in each case is even: 2 and 0.
19, 93 and 15 are odd because they cannot be divided by 2 exactly. Their last digits are 9, 3 and 5, which are odd numbers.

QUESTION: Find the missing numbers in the following sequence.
29, 27, 25, 23, __ , 19, 17, __ , 13.

ANSWER: This sequence is a sequence of odd numbers decreasing in steps of two. The missing numbers are 21 and 15.

QUESTION: Find the missing numbers in the following sequence.
12, 14, 16, __ , 20, 22, 24, __ , 28

ANSWER: The sequence is a set of even numbers increasing in steps of two. The missing numbers are 18 and 26.

Doubling

Whenever a number is multiplied by 2 the number is doubled.

Number	Multiply number by 2	Answer
2	2×2	4
4	2×4	8
7	2×7	14
22	2×22	44

QUESTION: Find the next number in the following sequence.
3, 6, 12, 24, __

ANSWER: Each number is being doubled (multiplied by 2). So the next number is $2 \times 24 = 48$.
3, 6, 12, 24, **48**

Halving

Whenever a number is divided by 2 it is halved.

Number	Divide number by 2	Answer
4	4 ÷ 2	2
8	8 ÷ 2	4
14	14 ÷ 2	7
44	44 ÷ 2	22

QUESTION: Find the next number in the following sequence.
128, 64, 32, _

ANSWER: Each number is being halved (divided by 2). So the next
number is 32 ÷ 2 = 16.
128, 64, 32, **16**

Rules

It is important to work out the rule that links each number in a
sequence with the next number.

QUESTION: What is the rule for the following number sequence?
1, 2, 4, 8, 16, 32, …

ANSWER: Double each number.

QUESTION: What is the rule for the following number sequence?
1, 3, 7, 15, 31, …

ANSWER: Double each number and add 1.

QUESTION: What is the rule for the following number sequence?
36, 33, 30, 27, 24, …

ANSWER: Subtract 3 from each number.

LEVEL 6

nth term

The rules of sequences can be shown using algebra. Algebra uses letters as symbols in formulae to show the rules. Each number in a sequence is called a term. As sequences can go on for many terms, a formula is written for finding any term in a sequence. Any missing term is called the nth term.

QUESTION: Write down a formula for the nth term of the following sequence, and work out what the 80th term would be. 3, 6, 9, 12, 15, …

ANSWER:

Term	1st	2nd	3rd	4th	5th	…	nth
Sequence	3	6	9	12	15	…	$3n$

Each term is multiplied by 3.
3×1 (1st term) = 3, 3×2 (2nd term) = 6, and so on.
nth term = $3n$
So the 80th term = $3 \times 80 = 240$.

QUESTION: Write down the formula for the nth term in the following sequence, and work out the 16th term. 4, 7, 10, 13, 16, …

ANSWER:

Term	1st	2nd	3rd	4th	5th	…	nth
Sequence	4	7	10	13	16	…	$3n + 1$

nth term = $3n + 1$

So the 16th term = $3 \times 16 + 1 = 48 + 1 = 49$.

×	1	2	3	4	5	6
1	1	2	3	4	5	
2	2	4	6	8	10	
3	3	6	9	12	15	
4	4	8	12	16	20	
5	5	10	15	20	25	
6						36

Multiplication grids

Multiplication grids contain rows, columns and diagonals with number patterns. If you look at the shaded leading diagonal in the grid below, the numbers form a sequence: 1, 4, 9, 16, 25

The numbers are increasing by 3, 5, 7, 9, so the next number will increase by 11: $25 + 11 = 36$.

QUESTION: Complete the multiplication grids.

2	4		8
3	6	9	

36	42		54
42		56	63

27	36		54
30		50	60

ANSWER:

2	4	**6**	8
3	6	9	**12**

36	42	**48**	54
42	**49**	56	63

27	36	**45**	54
30	**40**	50	60

Multiples

Whenever a number is multiplied by 2 the result is a multiple of 2. If a number is multiplied by 3 then the result is a multiple of 3, and so on.

For example:

$1 \times 2 = 2$

$2 \times 2 = 4$

$3 \times 2 = 6$

$4 \times 2 = 8$

2, 4, 6 and 8 are multiples of 2.

$10 \times 3 = 30$

$12 \times 3 = 36$

$14 \times 3 = 42$

30, 36 and 42 are multiples of 3.

A number can be a multiple of more than one number.
For example, 12 is a multiple of 2, 3, 4 and 6 because:

$6 \times 2 = 12$ (a multiple of 2)

$4 \times 3 = 12$ (a multiple of 3)

$3 \times 4 = 12$ (a multiple of 4)

$2 \times 6 = 12$ (a multiple of 6)

The following rules are worth knowing:

- Any even number is a multiple of 2.
- Any number with 5 as a last digit is a multiple of 5.
- Any number with 0 as a last digit will be a multiple of 5 and 10.

QUESTION: What are the multiples of 6 between 24 and 48?

ANSWER: 30, 36, 42

QUESTION: What are the multiples of 5 between 24 and 47?

ANSWER: 25, 30, 35, 40, 45

QUESTION: Which of the following numbers are not multiples of 4?
8, 12, 15, 17, 20

ANSWER: 15 and 17 are not multiples of 4.

Co-ordinates

In the diagram the rectangle ABCD has co-ordinates A(1,1), B(7,1), C(7,3), D(1,3). The first number in each co-ordinate refers to the number along the horizontal axis. The second number in each co-ordinate refers to the number along the vertical axis.

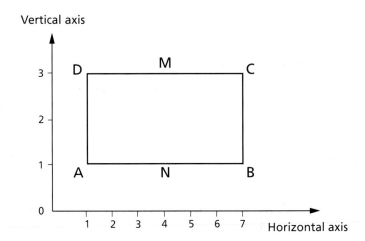

The letter M is half-way between C and D. So the co-ordinate of M is (4,3). The letter N is also half-way between A and D. The co-ordinate of N is (4,1).

Graphs

Graphs are a good way of showing the relationship between numbers. The graph shown has a point on it. The point ✕ is at (4,3). (4,3) are the co-ordinates of ✕. Always read along the x-axis (horizontal axis) first and then along the y-axis (vertical axis).

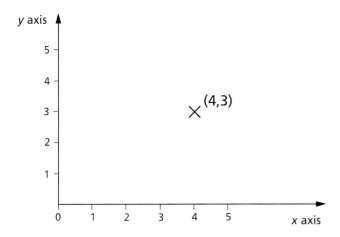

QUESTION: Draw a graph of the multiples of 3.

ANSWER: First draw a table and list a few numbers in the sequence, starting with zero.

Number	0	1	2	3	4
Multiple of 3	0	3	6	9	12

The pairs of numbers in the table can be plotted as co-ordinates on a graph: (0,0) (1,3) (2,6) (3,9) (4,12).

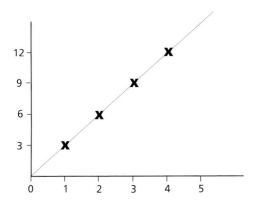

Factors

The factors of a number *N* are the set of numbers that can be multiplied by each other to give *N*. For example,

The factors of 4 are 1, 2 and 4 because:

$1 \times 4 = 4$

$4 \times 1 = 4$

$2 \times 2 = 4$

The table shows the factors of numbers between 4 and 8.

Number		Factors
4	$1 \times 4 = 4$	1, 2, 4
	$2 \times 2 = 4$	
	$4 \times 1 = 4$	
5	$1 \times 5 = 5$	1, 5
	$5 \times 1 = 5$	
6	$1 \times 6 = 6$	1, 2, 3, 6
	$6 \times 1 = 6$	
	$3 \times 2 = 6$	
	$2 \times 3 = 6$	
7	$1 \times 7 = 7$	1, 7
	$7 \times 1 = 7$	
8	$1 \times 8 = 8$	1, 2, 4, 8
	$8 \times 1 = 8$	
	$4 \times 2 = 8$	
	$2 \times 4 = 8$	

QUESTION: What are the factors of 15?

ANSWER:

$1 \times 15 = 15$

$3 \times 5 \ = 15$

$5 \times 3 \ = 15$

$15 \times 1 = 15$

So the factors of 15 are 15, 5, 3, and 1.

QUESTION: Write down multiplications replacing the symbols ∇, O for numbers.

O × ∇ = 18

ANSWER:

9 × 2 = 18	3 × 6 = 18
2 × 9 = 18	18 × 1 = 18
6 × 3 = 18	1 × 18 = 18

QUESTION: What are the factors of 20?

ANSWER:

1 × 20 = 20	5 × 4 = 20
2 × 10 = 20	10 × 2 = 20
4 × 5 = 20	20 × 1 = 20

So the factors of 20 are 20, 10, 5, 4, 2 and 1.

Squares

When a number is multiplied by itself the result is a square number. The diagram shows the relationship between the name 'square' and what the square of a number is.

The square of a number is given the symbol ^{2}.

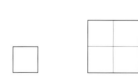

1 × 1 = 1   2 × 2 = 4   3 × 3 = 9

The table shows the squares of the numbers between 1 and 6.

Number	Number squared	Written as	Answer
1	1 × 1 =	1^2	1
2	2 × 2 =	2^2	4
3	3 × 3 =	3^2	9
4	4 × 4 =	4^2	16
5	5 × 5 =	5^2	25
6	6 × 6 =	6^2	36

QUESTION: How many balls would there be in the next pattern?

ANSWER: 16. The balls form a sequence of square numbers.

QUESTIONS: What is the square of the following numbers?
7, 8, 9, 10

ANSWERS:

$7^2 = 7 \times 7 = 49$

$8^2 = 8 \times 8 = 64$

$9^2 = 9 \times 9 = 81$

$10^2 = 10 \times 10 = 100$

Square roots

The square root of a number is the opposite, or inverse operation, of the square of a number. For example, $5^2 = 25$ so the square root of 25 is 5. The symbol for square root is $\sqrt{\ }$. $4^2 = 16$, so $\sqrt{16} = 4$. The square roots of some common square numbers are given below.

$\sqrt{1} = 1$	$\sqrt{36} = 6$
$\sqrt{4} = 2$	$\sqrt{49} = 7$
$\sqrt{9} = 3$	$\sqrt{64} = 8$
$\sqrt{16} = 4$	$\sqrt{81} = 9$
$\sqrt{25} = 5$	$\sqrt{100} = 10$

QUESTION: If $23^2 = 529$, what is $\sqrt{529}$?

ANSWER: As the square root is the opposite of squaring, $\sqrt{529} = 23$.

QUESTION: If $\sqrt{1024} = 32$ what is 32^2?

ANSWER: $32^2 = 1024$.

Cubes

When a number is multiplied by itself three times the result is a cube number. The diagrams show the relationship between the name 'cube' and what the cube of a number is.

$1 \times 1 \times 1 = 1$ $2 \times 2 \times 2 = 8$ $3 \times 3 \times 3 = 27$

The cube of a number is given the symbol ^{3}.

The table shows the cubes of the numbers between 1 and 6.

Number	Number cubed	Written as	Answer
1	$1 \times 1 \times 1 =$	1^3	1
2	$2 \times 2 \times 2 =$	2^3	8
3	$3 \times 3 \times 3 =$	3^3	27
4	$4 \times 4 \times 4 =$	4^3	64
5	$5 \times 5 \times 5 =$	5^3	125
6	$6 \times 6 \times 6 =$	6^3	216

QUESTION: What is the cube of the following numbers?
7, 8, 10

ANSWER:
$7 \times 7 \ = 49$
$49 \times 7 = 343$
So $7^3 = 343$

$8 \times 8 \ = 64$
$64 \times 8 = 512$
So $8^3 = 512$

$10 \times 10 \ = 100$
$100 \times 10 = 1000$
So $10^3 \ = 1000$

Prime numbers

A prime number is a number with only two factors, 1 and the number itself.

The table shows which numbers between 2 and 8 are prime numbers.

Number		Factors	Prime number	Reason
2	$1 \times 2 = 2$ $2 \times 1 = 2$	1, 2	Yes	2 is a prime number because 1 and 2 are the only factors
3	$1 \times 3 = 3$ $3 \times 1 = 3$	1, 3	Yes	3 is a prime number because 1 and 3 are the only factors
4	$1 \times 4 = 4$ $2 \times 2 = 4$ $4 \times 1 = 4$	1, 2, 4	No	4 is not a prime number because 2 is a factor as well as 1 and 4
5	$1 \times 5 = 5$ $5 \times 1 = 5$	1, 5	Yes	5 is a prime number because 1 and 5 are the only factors
6	$1 \times 6 = 6$ $6 \times 1 = 6$ $3 \times 2 = 6$ $2 \times 3 = 6$	1, 2, 3, 6	No	6 is not a prime number because 2 and 3 are factors as well as 1 and 6
7	$1 \times 7 = 7$ $7 \times 1 = 7$	1, 7	Yes	7 is a prime number because 1 and 7 are the only factors
8	$1 \times 8 = 8$ $8 \times 1 = 8$ $4 \times 2 = 8$ $2 \times 4 = 8$	1, 2, 4, 8	No	8 is not a prime number because 2 and 4 are factors as well as 1 and 8

The prime numbers are 2, 3, 5, 7, 11, 13, 17, 19, 23, 29, 31, 37, 41, 43 ... The number of prime numbers is endless.

QUESTION: Which of the following numbers are prime numbers?
67, 70, 72, 75, 79, 89

ANSWER:
70 and 72 are even numbers, they are multiples of 2.
75 is a multiple of 5.
67, 79 and 89 cannot be divided by any other number except 1 and themselves, so they are prime numbers.

CHAPTER 4

Algebra

Mappings

A mapping involves:

- an input value (for example a number)
- an operation (for example addition, subtraction, multiplication or division)
- an output value (for example a number)

A number machine is often used to describe operations on numbers. The diagrams are examples of number machines showing inputs, operations and the outputs.

Input   Operation   Output

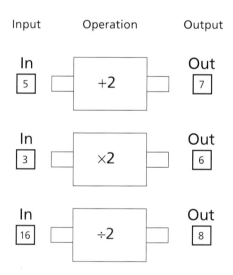

Inverse operations

If you know the relationships between numbers it is possible to work backwards from an output number to find out the input number.
For example:

Because we know that

$4 \times 7 = 28$, we also know that

$28 \div 7 = 4$

$28 \div 4 = 7$

QUESTION: Work out the inputs for the following operations and outputs.

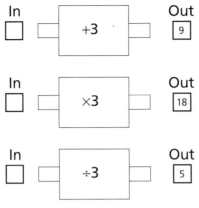

In ☐ → +3 → Out 9

In ☐ → ×3 → Out 18

In ☐ → ÷3 → Out 5

ANSWER: 6, 6, 15.

Sometimes the number machine may have more than one operation.

QUESTION: Using this number machine, complete the following table.

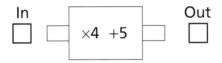

In ☐ → ×4 +5 → Out ☐

In	Out
2	
4	
	13
	29

ANSWER:

In	×4	+5	Out
2	8	13	13
4	16	21	21

Out	−5	÷4	In
13	8	2	2
29	24	6	6

So the completed table is

In	Out
2	13
4	21
2	13
6	29

Simple formulae

In algebra numbers are often represented by letters. If any two numbers p and q are multiplied, then instead of writing $p \times q$ it is usual to write pq. If p is divided by q, then instead of writing $p \div q$ it is usual to write $\frac{p}{q}$.

For example, the area (A) of a rectangle can be worked out using the formula:

$A = lw$ where l = length

w = width

l length

w width

The main advantage of using the formula in the example above is that it allows you to work out the area of any rectangle.

QUESTION: Using the formula above for the area of a rectangle, work out the measurements for each of these rectangles.

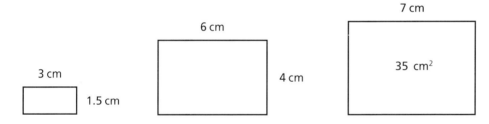

3 cm

1.5 cm

6 cm

4 cm

7 cm

35 cm²

ANSWER:

Using $A = lw$

- The area of the first rectangle is $3 \times 1.5 = 4.5$ cm²
- The area of the second rectangle is $6 \times 4 = 24$ cm²
- The width of the third rectangle is calculated from $w = \frac{A}{l}$, so $w = \frac{35}{7}$ cm = 5 cm.

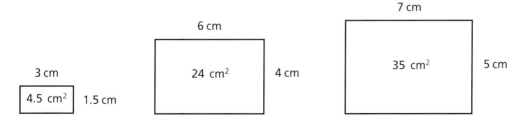

3 cm

4.5 cm²   1.5 cm

6 cm

24 cm²   4 cm

7 cm

35 cm²   5 cm

QUESTION: Work out a formula for the perimeter of a square of side length *l*.

l

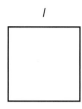

ANSWER: The perimeter of a square is the total of the lengths of each side. Each side is of length *l*, so the perimeter of any square can be written as 4*l*.

QUESTION: If there are *n* items and the cost of each item is 20p, write down a formula for the total cost C in pence of all the items.

ANSWER: C = 20*n*

QUESTION: Write down a formula for the cost, C, in pence of *n* sweets when one sweet costs 2p.

ANSWER: C = 2*n*

QUESTION: If *x* sweets cost 58p, write down a formula for the cost in pence of one sweet.

ANSWER:

x sweets cost 58pence

1 sweet costs $\dfrac{58}{x}$ pence

QUESTION: Write down a formula for the cost, C, of *y* sweets each costing *q* pence.

ANSWER: C = *yq*

QUESTION: A girl hires a cycle from the local park. The price charged for the hire is £2, plus 50p per hour borrowed. If *h* represents hours hired and C represents the total cost of hire in pence, write down a formula for the total cost, C, in terms of *h*. If the total cost came to £4, how many hours did the girl hire the cycle for?

ANSWER:

Convert the pounds into pence. £2 = 200p.

C = 200 + 50*h*

If C = 400 then:

400 = 200 + 50*h*

50*h* = 200

h = 4 hours.

Linear equations

A simple linear equation usually involves one unknown number, called a variable, which is represented by a letter. For example, $x + 5 = 12$ is a linear equation. Solving a linear equation means finding the value of x that fits, or satisfies, the equation. In this example, $x = 7$, because $7 + 5 = 12$.

QUESTION: Find the value of x for the equation $x + 12 = 19$.

ANSWER: $x = 7$, because $7 + 12 = 19$.

QUESTION: Find the value of y for the equation $4 + y = 18$.

ANSWER: $y = 14$, because $4 + 14 = 18$.

QUESTION: If n is a number and $n + 5 = 14$, what is the value of $n + 8$?

ANSWER: $n = 9$, because $9 + 5 = 14$. So $n + 8 = 9 + 8 = 17$.

QUESTION: Find the value of t for the equation $3 - t = 12$.

ANSWER: $t = -9$ because $3 - (-9) = 3 + 9 = 12$
(remember 'two minuses make a plus').

Further linear equations

LEVEL 6

The steps involved in solving linear equations are always the same:

- The = sign acts like a weighing scale. If two sides of a weighing scale are balanced and you add a weight to one side then you have to add the same weight to the other side to keep it balanced. You can carry out an arithmetic operation on one side of the equation, provided the operation is repeated on the other side of the equation.

- The = separates two different sides of the equation. In order to solve a simple linear equation you must move the unknown value to one side of the equation and everything else to the other side of the equation.

The examples below illustrate the steps involved in solving a linear equation.

QUESTION: Solve $x - 27 = 46$.

ANSWER:

Add 27 to both sides

$x - 27 + 27 = 46 + 27$

$\qquad$ ($-27 + 27 = 0$ and $46 + 27 = 73$, so)

$x + 0 = 73$

$x = 73$

QUESTION: Solve $3x - 1 = x + 5$.

ANSWER:

Move the unknowns to one side, so subtract x from both sides

$3x - 1 - x = x + 5 - x$

$\qquad$ ($3x - x = 2x$, and $x + (-x) = 0$, so)

$2x - 1 = 5$

Add 1 to both sides

$2x = 6$

Divide both sides by 2

$$\frac{2x}{2} = \frac{6}{3}$$

$x = 2$

QUESTION: Solve $7 - t = 3t + 3$.

ANSWER:

Add t to both sides

$7 - t + t = 3t + 3 + t$

$7 = 4t + 3$

Subtract 3 from both sides

$7 - 3 = 4t + 3 - 3$

$4 = 4t$

Divide both sides by 4

$$\frac{4}{4} = t$$

Or $t = 1$

QUESTION: Solve $4 + y = 9y - 2$.

ANSWER:

Subtract y from both sides

$4 + y - y = 9y - 2 - y$

$4 = 8y - 2$

Add 2 to both sides

$6 = 8y$

Divide both sides by 8

$$\frac{6}{8} = \frac{8y}{8}$$

or $y = \frac{3}{4}$

Trial and improvement

Trial and improvement is important because many equations in mathematics cannot be solved by algebra. The example shows the method of trial and improvement.

Solve the equation $x^2 = 20$.

x	x^2	Result	
4	4^2	16	Too small so try a number higher than 4
5	5^2	25	Too big so try a number between 4 and 5
4.5	4.5^2	20.25	Too big but close so try a number just below 4.5
4.45	4.45^2	19.8025	Too small so try a number between 4.45 and 4.5
4.475	4.475^2	20.02563	Too big so try a number just lower than 4.475
4.473	4.473^2	20.00773	This is close enough, but we could continue.

The accurate solution, using the square root function on a calculator, is 4.472136. Computers are often used to work out the answers to equations.

CHAPTER 5

Properties of shapes

Most objects in everyday life consist of one or more basic shapes. Shapes are grouped according to whether they are two-dimensional (2-D) or three dimensional (3-D). 2-D shapes are shapes that could be laid flat on a table. 3-D shapes are shapes that have a base and height. This chapter examines common basic shapes and their properties.

Lines

The most basic shape of all is the line. A line drawn straight 'across' is called a horizontal line.

Horizontal line

A line drawn straight 'up' or 'down' is called a vertical line.

Vertical line

When a horizontal line meets a vertical line the two lines are called perpendicular lines.

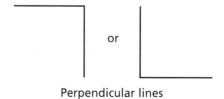

Perpendicular lines

Two lines drawn in the same direction but never meeting are called parallel lines.

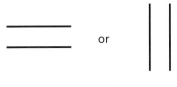

or

Parallel lines

A diagram of a typical door shows examples of all these types of lines.

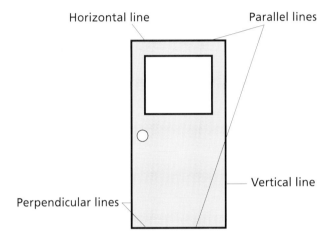

Horizontal line   Parallel lines

Vertical line

Perpendicular lines

Angles

An angle is a measure of a 'turn' between two lines. The angle between two perpendicular lines is called a right angle.

Angles are measured in degrees. The symbol for a degree is °. There are 90° in a right angle.

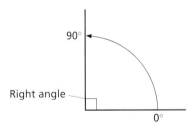

90°

Right angle

0°

The diagrams show a line as it turns through more than one right angle.

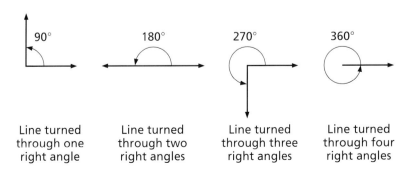

90°   180°   270°   360°

Line turned   Line turned   Line turned   Line turned
through one   through two   through three   through four
right angle   right angles   right angles   right angles

The relationships between angles and right angles are summarised in the table.

Line turned through	Angle
One right angle	90°
Two right angles	180°
Three right angles	270°
Four right angles	360°

When a line has been turned, it has been rotated through an angle. After rotating a line through four right angles the line ends up where it started. The line has turned through one complete circle or revolution. There are therefore 360° in one circle.

QUESTION: A pointer on a dial is turned. In each of the diagrams, how many right angles has it been turned through?

ANSWER: 1, 3 and 2.

There are special names given to some angles.

Angle	Name
Less than 90°	Acute
Greater than 90° but less than 180°	Obtuse
Between 180° and 360°	Reflex

Acute angle   Obtuse angle   Reflex angle

Angle relationships between parallel and intersecting lines

A line represents an angle of 180°. When two lines meet they intersect. Look at the intersecting lines below.

Two intersecting lines

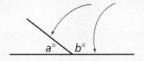

$a + b = 180°$

a and b are called supplementary angles

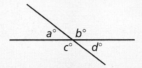

$a = d$ and $b = c$

a and d are called vertically opposite angles

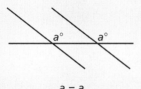

$a = a$

the two equal angles are called corresponding angles

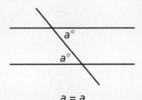

$a = a$

the two equal angles are called alternate angles (or Z angles)

QUESTIONS: Work out the angles x and y in the diagrams.

(a)

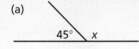

(b)

(c)

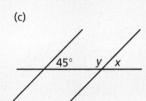

(d)

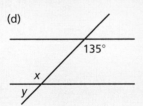

ANSWERS:

a) *x* and 45° are supplementary angles. There are 180° on a straight line so $x = 180° - 45 = 135°$.

b) *x* and 30° are vertically opposite angles, so $x = 30°$.

c) *x* and 45° are corresponding angles so $x = 45°$, *x* and *y* are supplementary angles, so $y = 180° - 45° = 135°$.

d) *x* and 135° are alternate angles, so $x = 135°$; *x* and *y* are supplementary angles so $y = 45°$

Two-dimensional (2-D) shapes

The simplest 2-D shape is the line.

Line

Triangles

Shapes with three sides are called triangles. Some triangles have special names.

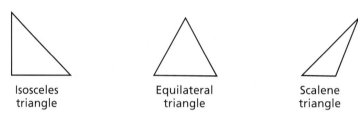

Isosceles
triangle

Equilateral
triangle

Scalene
triangle

Quadrilaterals

Shapes with four sides are called quadrilaterals. The most common quadrilaterals are shown in the diagrams.

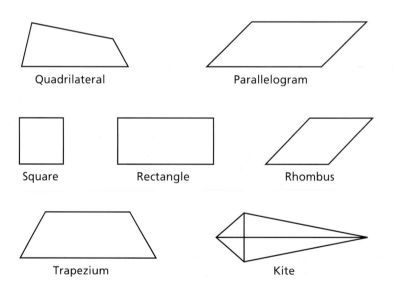

Quadrilateral

Parallelogram

Square

Rectangle

Rhombus

Trapezium

Kite

Polygons

The term 'poly' means 'many', so polygon is another word for 'many-sided shape'. The most common polygons are shown below. A regular polygon is a polygon with sides of equal length.

Regular
pentagon

Regular
hexagon

Regular
octagon

Circular shapes

The circle and semi-circle are two common circular shapes.

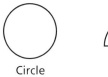

Circle   Semi-circle

The table shows some characteristics of different shapes.

Shape	Number of sides	Properties
Triangle	3	**Total of all angles in a triangle add up to 180°**
Equilateral		Three sides of equal length and three equal angles of 60°
Isosceles		Two sides of equal length and two equal angles
Scalene		Three sides of different length
Quadrilaterals	4	**Total of all angles in a quadrilateral add up to 360°**
Parallelograms		Opposite sides equal in length and parallel to each other
Square		Four sides of equal length and four right angles
Rectangle		Opposite sides of equal length and four right angles
Rhombus		Four sides of equal length. Opposite sides are parallel
Kite		Made up of two isosceles triangles
Trapezium		Two sides are parallel
Regular polygons		**Many-sided shapes**
Pentagon	5	Five sides of equal length ('Pent' means 5)
Hexagon	6	Six sides of equal length ('Hex' means 6)
Octagon	8	Eight sides of equal length ('Oct' means 8)

Congruence

If a shape has been rotated or reflected the shape may not look the same. Shapes that do look the same even if they have been reflected or rotated are called congruent shapes. For example, the two shapes below are congruent because they are both squares, of the same size, but one has been rotated.

 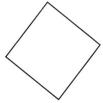

The shapes shown below are congruent because each shape can be rotated until it looks the same as the other two.

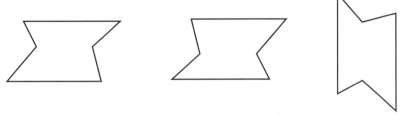

The shapes shown below are not congruent because they are of different sizes.

QUESTION: Which of the triangles are congruent?

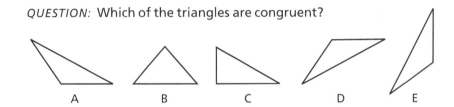

ANSWER: Triangles A, D and E are congruent. Triangles B and C are different shapes to A, D and E. They cannot be reflected or rotated to look the same as A, D and E.

Three-dimensional (3-D) shapes

Some common 3-D shapes are shown below.

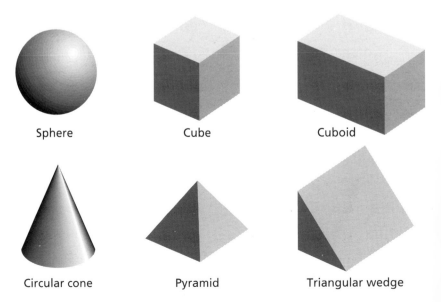

Sphere   Cube   Cuboid

Circular cone   Pyramid   Triangular wedge

Angle properties of regular polygons

The angle properties of regular (equal-sided) polygons (2-D shapes) are based on triangles. All the angles inside a triangle add up to 180°. Below are two common triangles.

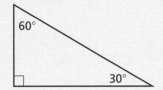

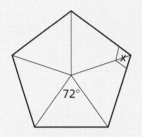

QUESTION: Find the angle x in the regular pentagon.

ANSWER: A regular pentagon is made up of five isosceles triangles.

There are 360° in one complete revolution or circle. So the angles around the centre O of the pentagon add up to 360°. As there are five equal sides there are five equal angles of 360° ÷ 5 = 72° at the centre of each triangle.

Because the angles in any triangle add up to 180°, the angles at the base of each triangle in the pentagon must be 54°. The angle *x* is two angles of 54° so it is 108°.

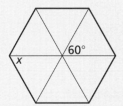

QUESTION: Find the angle *x* in the regular hexagon.

ANSWER: A regular hexagon is made up of six equilateral triangles.

There are six equal sides to a regular hexagon. So there are six equal angles of 60° (360 ÷ 6 = 60) at the centre of a hexagon.

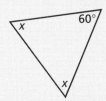

As there are 180° in any triangle then *2x* + 60 = 180. So *x* = 60°.

Nets

3-D shapes can be laid out flat as 2-D patterns. Flattened 3-D shapes are called nets. You can make nets out of cardboard. By folding cardboard nets you can create the 3-D shape. The examples show nets for a box and a pyramid with a square base.

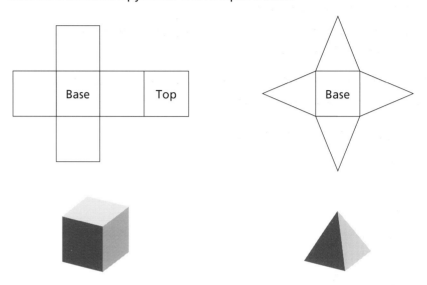

Some 3-D shapes can be made from many different nets. Three more examples of nets for the box are shown. Try making some yourself and see if you can work out any more.

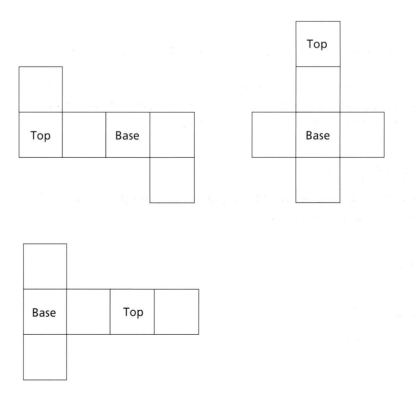

Reflection in a mirror line

It is possible to work out what a shape looks like when it is reflected in a mirror by:

- drawing an imaginary line on a piece of paper next to the shape
- imagining folding along the line
- imagining what the shape will look like when folded on to the other side of the line.

Example: The diagram shows what the letters C, E, R, T and F would look like when reflected in a mirror.

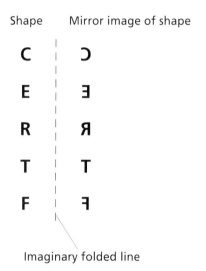

Imaginary folded line

Reflective symmetries of 2-D and 3-D shapes

When a shape looks the same after reflecting it about a line, which passes through the shape itself, the shape has a line of symmetry. Another name for a line of symmetry is a fold-line.

Lines of symmetry

Some of the 2-D shapes below have lines of symmetry. The lines of symmetry have been drawn on.

Lines

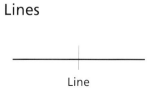

Line

Triangles

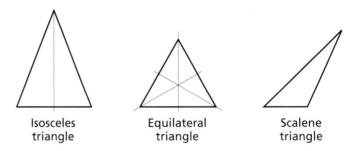

Isosceles
triangle

Equilateral
triangle

Scalene
triangle

Quadrilaterals

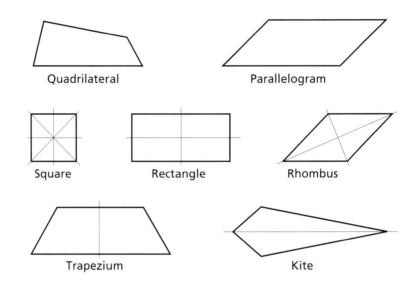

Quadrilateral

Parallelogram

Square

Rectangle

Rhombus

Trapezium

Kite

Polygons

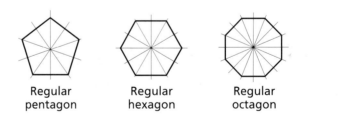

Regular
pentagon

Regular
hexagon

Regular
octagon

Circular shapes

The lines of symmetry of a circle are infinite (never ending).
Only a few have been shown.

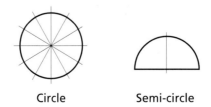

Circle

Semi-circle

The table shows how many lines of symmetry some shapes have.

Shape	Lines of symmetry
Triangles	
Equilateral	3
Isosceles	1
Scalene	0
Quadrilaterals	
Parallelograms	0
Square	4
Rectangle	2
Rhombus	2
Kite	1
Regular polygons	
Pentagon	5
Hexagon	6
Octagon	8
Circular shapes	
Circle	Infinite
Semi-circle	1

Vertical, horizontal or any line can be used as reflective lines.

QUESTION: Which capital letters of the alphabet have reflective symmetry about a vertical axis, and which have reflective symmetry about a horizontal axis?

ANSWER:

ABCDEFGHIJKLMN
OPQRSTUVWXYZ

Letters of the alphabet which have reflective
symmetry about a vertical axis

ABCDEFGHIJKLMN
OPQRSTUVWXYZ

Letters of the alphabet which have reflective
symmetry about a horizontal axis

3-D shapes planes of symmetry

3-D shapes do not have lines of symmetry but have planes of symmetry. A plane is the 3-D equivalent to a line. There may be many planes of symmetry, but just two planes of symmetry are shown here for a cube and a rectangular block.

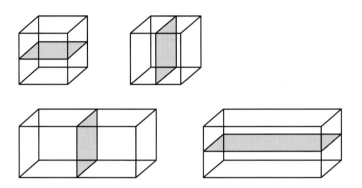

The sphere has an infinite (never ending) range of planes of symmetry. Just one plane has been drawn.

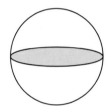

Rotational symmetry of 2-D shapes

Some shapes do not have symmetry about a line, but they have another type of symmetry called rotational symmetry. If a shape can be rotated about an axis perpendicular to the shape, and it looks the same before returning to it's original position, then the figure has rotational symmetry.

For example, imagine a table with a rectangular sheet of paper lying on it. From afar the table and paper would look like this:

Line or axis perpendicular to the table and shape

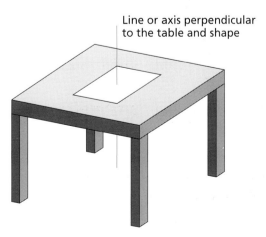

If you look down on the rectangular sheet of paper and ignore the table then it would like this:

The circle represents the imaginary axis about which the paper could be rotated. If the corners of the rectangle are labelled A, B, C and D and it is rotated through 180°, the shape looks identical. The rectangle has rotational symmetry.

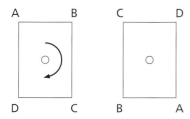

The number of times a shape can be rotated, including the last turn, and look the same as its original position is called the order of symmetry. For example, the rectangle above has rotational symmetry of order 2.

A square has rotational symmetry of order 4, because the square can be rotated four times and look the same as its original position.

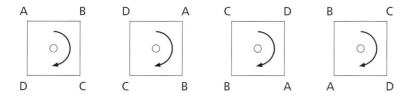

A square has rotational symmetry of order 4

QUESTION: Which of the following shapes have rotational symmetry and what is their order of symmetry?

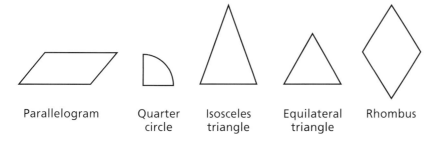

Parallelogram   Quarter circle   Isosceles triangle   Equilateral triangle   Rhombus

ANSWER:
The equilateral triangle has rotational symmetry of order 3.
The rhombus has rotational symmetry of order 2.

Example: The order of symmetry for each shape below is given.

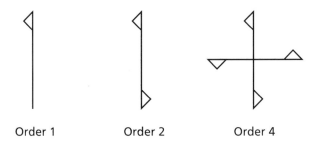

Order 1   Order 2   Order 4

QUESTION: Which of these letters have rotational symmetry, and what is their order of symmetry?

X U I O B Z M N S H

ANSWER:
X has rotational symmetry of order 2.
I has rotational symmetry of order 2.
Z has rotational symmetry of order 2.
S has rotational symmetry of order 2.
H has rotational symmetry of order 2.
O has rotational symmetry of an infinite (never ending) order.
The letter O may be rotated over and over and it will always look the same.

QUESTION: A simple jig-saw is shown. How many different ways can each piece fit into its hole?

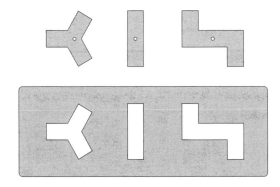

ANSWER:

The first piece has rotational symmetry of order 3 so it can be placed into its hole in three different ways.

The second piece has rotational symmetry of order 2 so it can be placed into its hole in two different ways.

The third piece has rotational symmetry of order 2 so it can be placed into its hole in two different ways.

Isometric drawings

Isometric drawings are a way of drawing 3-D shapes on 2-D paper. Using the isometric drawing of an object, you can draw the shape of the object as seen from the top, front and side views.

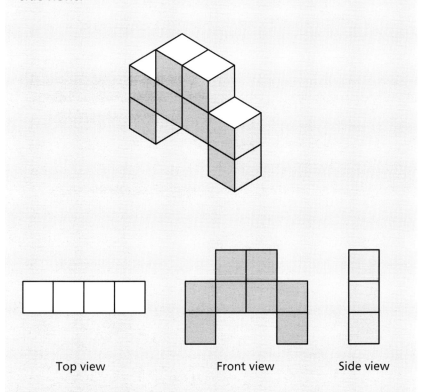

Top view   Front view   Side view

CHAPTER 6

Properties of position and movement

Co-ordinate systems

Co-ordinate systems are a way of working out where an object or shape is located. For example, co-ordinates can be used to find the position of buildings on a map, aircraft in the sky and satellites in space. This chapter examines some simple co-ordinate systems.

Location by direction

One of the oldest ways of finding an object is to use direction.

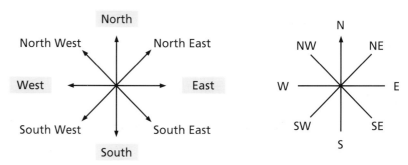

QUESTION: Using the compass directions above, describe the journey from the house to Churchlawns school.

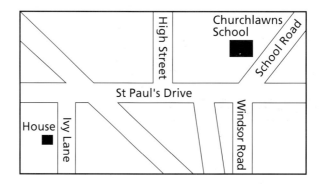

ANSWER:
Go north (N) up Ivy Lane.
Then go east (E) along St Paul's Drive.
Then go north-east (NE) along School Road.

Location by grid reference

Grid references use rows (which are horizontal) and columns (which are vertical) to tell where an object is. The rows are usually given numbers and the columns are usually given letters of the alphabet. To find out where an object is on a grid:

- Read along each column until you reach the column the object is above.

- Read along each row until you reach the one the object is along.

QUESTION: Work out the grid reference for each shape in the diagram.

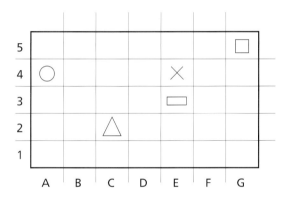

ANSWER:

The circle is at grid reference A4.   The cross is at grid reference E4.

The triangle is at grid reference C2.   The square is at grid reference G5.

The rectangle is at grid reference E3.

QUESTION: In which square of the diagram is the house located? In which square is the school located? Which building can be found in C2?

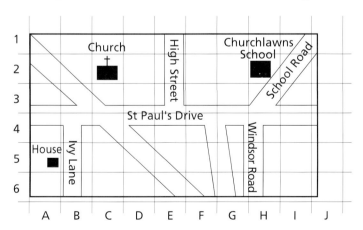

ANSWER:

The house is at A5.   The school is at H2.   The church is at C2.

Other types of grid reference use numbers for both the horizontal rows and vertical columns.

QUESTION: Work out the grid reference for each shape in the diagram.

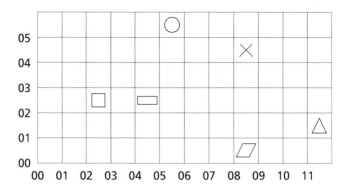

ANSWER:

Shape	Grid reference	Shape	Grid reference
Square	0202	Cross	0804
Rectangle	0402	Parallelogram	0800
Circle	0505	Triangle	1101

Co-ordinate maps

Objects can be found by using co-ordinate maps. The first number of each co-ordinate refers to the horizontal axis and the second number of the co-ordinate refers to the vertical axis.

QUESTION: Using the co-ordinate map, write down the co-ordinates of each letter.

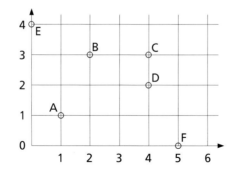

ANSWER:

Letter	Co-ordinate	Letter	Co-ordinate
A	(1,1)	D	(4,2)
B	(2,3)	E	(0,4)
C	(4,3)	F	(5,0)

QUESTION: Mark these points on a grid, join them up in order and colour in the shape drawn.

(1,3) then (3,5) then (5,3) then (3,1).

ANSWER:

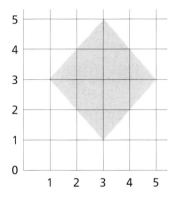

QUESTION: Using the co-ordinate map, write down the co-ordinates of each letter.

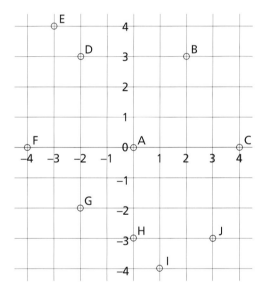

ANSWER:

Letter	Co-ordinate	Letter	Co-ordinate
A	(0,0)	F	(–4,0)
B	(2,3)	G	(–2,–2)
C	(4,0)	H	(0,–3)
D	(–2,3)	I	(1,–4)
E	(–3,4)	J	(3,–3)

QUESTION: You have been given the co-ordinates of some shapes. Mark these co-ordinates on a grid.

Shape	Co-ordinates
Square	(−3,2) (−3,4) (−1,2) (−1,4)
Rectangle	(−2,3) (2,3) (−2,−2) (2,−2)
Triangle	(2,2) (4,2) (3,4)

ANSWER:

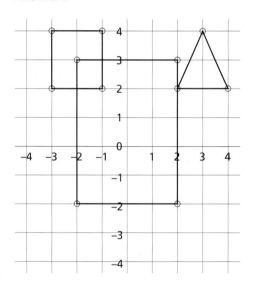

Transformation of 2-D shapes

Shapes can be made to look different by:

- translating them
- reflecting them
- rotating them

Translation

When a shape moves from one position to another by sliding the shape in any direction then the shape has been translated. The shape has not been turned round or flipped.

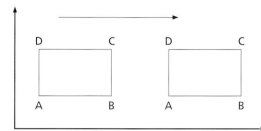

In the diagram the rectangle has been translated from one position to another position. When the rectangle slides along from the left to the right each co-ordinate is changed.

Reflection

When a shape is reflected in a line then the shape will appear in a different place and can look different.

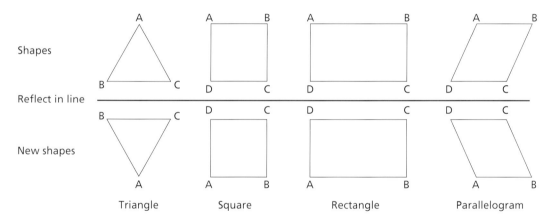

Rotation

Any object can be rotated by turning it around a point. Imagine placing a pencil through a shape and turning the shape around the fixed pencil. When a shape turns about a point the shape can look different.

A shape can be rotated by a turn, a right angle, or a degree. The table shows how rotation can be described in different ways, using the letter E as an example.

Letter E rotated by:	Turn	Right angles	Degrees
E	0	0	0
m	$\frac{1}{4}$	1	90
∃	$\frac{1}{2}$	2	180
ш	$\frac{3}{4}$	3	270
E	1	4	360

Rotation by turns

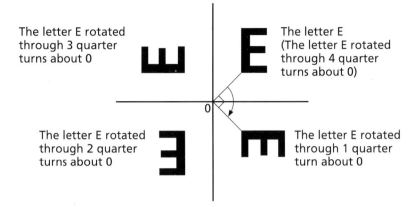

The letter E rotated through 3 quarter turns about 0

The letter E (The letter E rotated through 4 quarter turns about 0)

The letter E rotated through 2 quarter turns about 0

The letter E rotated through 1 quarter turn about 0

Rotation by right angles

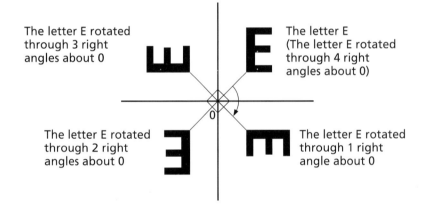

The letter E rotated through 3 right angles about 0

The letter E (The letter E rotated through 4 right angles about 0)

The letter E rotated through 2 right angles about 0

The letter E rotated through 1 right angle about 0

Rotation by degrees

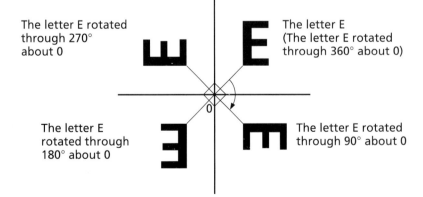

The letter E rotated through 270° about 0

The letter E (The letter E rotated through 360° about 0)

The letter E rotated through 180° about 0

The letter E rotated through 90° about 0

Example:
The diagrams show how a triangle looks after rotating it through different angles.

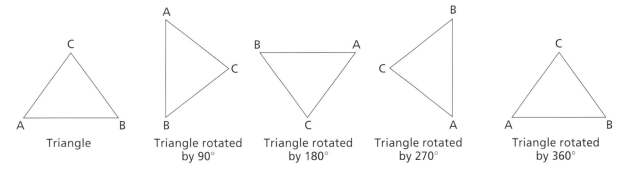

Example:
The next diagrams show how a rectangle would look after rotating it through different angles.

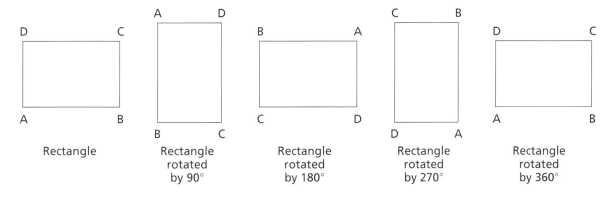

LEVEL 6

Enlargement

To make a shape larger, you can use a scale factor. The scale factor of an enlargement tells you 'how many times larger' the shape will become. For example, if a shape is to be enlarged by a scale factor of two then the shape will become twice as large. If the scale factor is three, then the shape will become three times as large.

When enlarging a shape you have to consider two things:

- the centre of enlargement (where the measurements start from), which can be inside or outside the shape
- the scale factor (the amount of times larger the shape will become)

QUESTION: A square with corners A, B, C and D is to be enlarged by a scale factor of 2. O, the centre of enlargement, is outside the shape to be enlarged. Draw the new shape.

ANSWER:
Measure the length of the lines between O and A, O and B, O and C, O and D.
Multiply each length by 2 (the scale factor).
Draw the new shape, and label the corners A′, B′, C′ and D′.

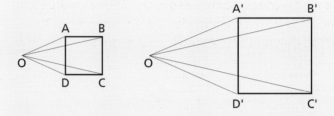

QUESTION: A square with corners A, B, C and D is to be enlarged by a scale factor of 2. O, the centre of enlargement is inside the shape to be enlarged. Draw the new shape.

ANSWER:
Measure the length of the lines between O and A, O and B, O and C, O and D.
Multiply each length by 2 (the scale factor).
Draw the new shape, and label the corners A′, B′, C′ and D′.

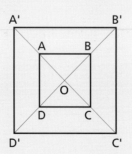

CHAPTER 7

Measures

Units of length, mass, capacity and time

Every day you have to deal with lengths, masses, capacities and time. To measure these quantities easily, we use units.

Some words, called prefixes, can be used with different units. Each prefix has a meaning that is the same for the different units. The table shows three common prefixes and their meanings.

Prefix	Meaning	Called
milli	$\frac{1}{1000}$ th	one thousandth
centi	$\frac{1}{100}$ th	one hundredth
kilo	1000	one thousand

Length

The table shows the common metric units used for measuring length or distance. The basic metric unit of length is the metre (m).

Unit	Symbol	Meaning	Used for	Examples
millimetres	mm	$\frac{1}{1000}$ th of a metre	Very small lengths	Length of an ant, thickness of a mirror, length of a tip of a short fingernail
centimetres	cm	$\frac{1}{100}$ th of a metre	Small lengths	Length of a pen, length of babies, length of a child's fingernail
metres	m	One unit of length	Medium lengths	Height of adults, height of a tree, length of cars
kilometres	km	1000 metres	Large lengths	Distance to the town centre, distance between two towns, distances to planets and the Sun

Mass (weight)

Weight is the term often used to describe the mass of an object. The basic metric unit of mass is the gram (g). The table shows the common metric units for measuring mass.

Unit	Symbol	Meaning	Used for	Examples
grams	g	One unit of mass	Light weights	Food items such as packets of biscuits, crisps, chocolate bars
kilograms	kg	1000 grams	Medium weights	A person's weight, a bag of sugar, a bag of potatoes
tonnes	t	1000 kilograms	Heavy weights	A bus, an aeroplane, an elephant

Capacity (volume)

Volume is another term for capacity. The basic metric unit of capacity is the cubic metre, m^3. The volume of liquids is usually expressed in litres (l).

Unit	Symbol	Meaning	Used for	Examples
millilitres	ml	$\frac{1}{1000}$ th of a litre	Very small volumes	A spoonful of medicine (using 5 ml spoons), a glass of juice
centilitres	cl	$\frac{1}{100}$ th of a litre	Small volumes	A small bottle of juice
litres	l	One unit of volume	Large volumes	A large bottle of fizzy drink, a tank of petrol

Time

The basic unit of time is the second (s).

Unit	Symbol	Meaning	Used for	Examples
milliseconds	ms	$\frac{1}{1000}$ th of a second	Very short times	Parts of a second during races
seconds	s	One unit of time	Short times	100 m sprint race
minutes	min	60 seconds	Medium times	Duration of maths lesson
hours	h	60 minutes	Long times	Duration of a train journey

Estimates of measures in everyday life

You can estimate amounts of unknown quantities by comparing the unknown quantity to a known value. For example, we know that a very tall man is about 2 m high, so we can estimate the height of everyday objects by comparing them with the height of a tall man.

Below some everyday objects are used as examples of certain units. If you remember the examples, you can use them to estimate the length, mass or capacity of other objects and to estimate time.

Length

millimetres (mm)

The length of the tip of a short fingernail is about 1 mm.

Fingernail — Tip of fingernail approximately 1 mm

You can estimate the length of very small objects by comparing them with the length of the tip of a fingernail.

centimetres (cm)

The length of a child's fingernail is about 1 cm.

Fingernail approximately 1 cm — Tip of fingernail

By keeping a mental picture of 1 cm on a ruler, it is quite easy to estimate the lengths of drawn lines.

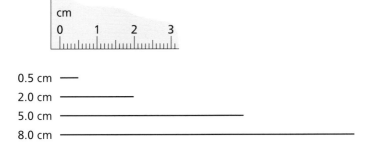

cm
0   1   2   3

0.5 cm ——
2.0 cm ——————
5.0 cm ————————————————
8.0 cm ————————————————————————

metres (m)

The average height of a 10–11 year old is 1.35 m (or 135 cm). So the heights of everyday objects such as tables and other objects in a room can be compared with this height.

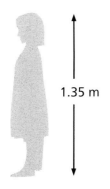

1.35 m

10–11 year old

Mass

grams (g)

A chocolate sweet is about 1 g in weight.

An ordinary-sized loaf of bread is about 800 g in weight.

kilograms (kg)

An ordinary-sized packet of sugar is about 1 kg in weight.

tonnes (t)

An average-sized elephant weighs about 5 tonnes (5000 kg).

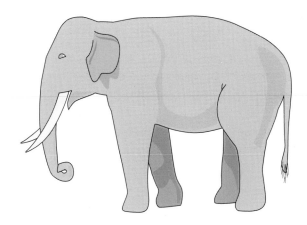

Capacity

millilitres (ml)

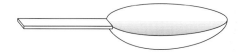

A medicine spoon holds around 5 ml of liquid.

centilitres (cl)

A standard bottle of wine holds about 75 cl (750 ml).

litres (l)

A family-sized bottle of fizzy drink holds about 2 l.

Time

seconds (s)

When parachutists dive from an aeroplane they have to wait for a certain number of seconds before opening their parachutes. To count the number of seconds they can say to themselves 'One one thousand, two one thousand, three one thousand …', and so on. It takes approximately 1 s to say the words 'one one thousand'.

minutes (min)

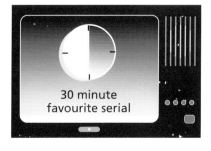

The length of an episode of many popular serials on television is about 30 min.

hours (h)

The length of a film on the television, or on video or at the cinema is usually about 1.5 to 2 h.

Measuring instruments

Many instruments have been designed to measure different types of quantities. When you choose a measuring instrument you have to think about how accurate you want your answer to be. A measuring instrument usually has a scale. The accuracy of the scale depends on the reason for which the instrument was designed.

For example, a watch or clock is a suitable time measuring instrument to measure the length of a journey. However, a more accurate time measuring instrument, such as a stopwatch, is needed to time a sprint race over 100 m.

The table lists the examples of instruments and how accurate or precise they are.

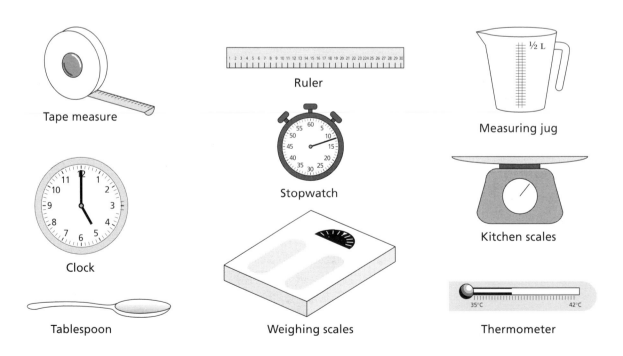

Tape measure

Ruler

Measuring jug

Clock

Stopwatch

Kitchen scales

Tablespoon

Weighing scales

Thermometer

Instrument	Measures	Units/scale	Precision
Tape measure	Length	0–1.5 m	To the nearest mm
Ruler	Length	0–30 cm	To the nearest mm
Measuring jug	Capacity (volume)	$0-\frac{1}{2}$ l	To the nearest 50 ml
Clock (no seconds)	Time	min to h	To the nearest min
Stopwatch	Time	s	To the nearest s
Kitchen weighing scales	Mass (weight)	0–2.2 kg	To the nearest 25 g
Tablespoon (15 ml)	Capacity (volume)	ml	15 ml
Thermometer	Temperature	35°C–42°C	To the nearest $\frac{1}{10}$ °C
Weighing scales	Mass (weight)	0–120 kg	To the nearest 1 kg

Converting units

Sometimes you have to be able to change from one unit to another unit. When converting units, it is best to write down the relationship between the units to be changed first.

Length

QUESTION: How many centimetres in 0.5 km?

ANSWER:

1 km   = 1000 m and 100 cm = 1 m
0.5 km = 0.5 × 1000 m
        = 500 m
        = 500 × 100 cm
        = 50000 cm

QUESTION: How many millimetres in 7.5 m?

ANSWER:

1 m   = 100 cm and 1 cm = 10 mm
7.5 m = 7.5 × 100 cm
        = 750 cm
        = 10 × 750 mm
        = 7500 mm

Mass (Weight)

QUESTION: How many grams are there in 2.3 kg?

ANSWER:

1 kg	=	1000 g
2.3 × 1 kg	=	2.3 × 1000 g
2.3 kg	=	2300 g

QUESTION: How many grams are there in 0.5 kg?

ANSWER:

1 kg	=	1000 g
0.5 × 1 kg	=	0.5 × 1000 g
0.5 kg	=	500 g

QUESTION: How many kilograms is 275 g?

ANSWER:

1000 g	=	1 kg
1 g	=	$\frac{1}{1000}$ kg
275 g	=	$\frac{275}{1000}$ kg
275 g	=	0.275 kg

QUESTION: How many kilograms are there in 7.6 t?

ANSWER:

1 t	=	1000 kg
7.6 × 1 t	=	7.6 × 1000 kg
7.6 t	=	7600 kg

Capacity

QUESTION: How many millilitres are there in 3.5 l?

ANSWER:

1 l	=	1000 ml
3.5 l	=	3.5 × 1000 ml
3.5 l	=	3500 ml

QUESTION: A person orders 12 bottles of wine. Each bottle of wine contains 75 cl. How many litres of wine will be delivered?

ANSWER:

1 l	=	100 cl
12 bottles of wine	=	12 × 75 cl
	=	900 cl
	=	9 l

Time

QUESTION: How many seconds in 2.5 min?

ANSWER:

1 min   =   60 s

2.5 min   = 2.5×60 s

=   150 s

QUESTION: A film lasts 128 min. Express this in hours and minutes.

ANSWER:

1 h   =   60 min

2 h   =   120 min

128 min   =   2 hours and 8 minutes

Converting Imperial units to metric units

Many countries only use the metric system to measure units. The metric system is based on units of ten. In the United Kingdom we use two sets of units, metric units and Imperial units. It is possible to convert metric units to Imperial units, and Imperial units to metric units. Approximations make the conversions easier.

Imperial unit	Approximate equivalent metric unit
1 inch	2.54 cm
1 foot (12 inches)	30 cm
1 yard (3 feet)	1 m
5 miles	8 km
2 pounds (lb)	1 kg
1.75 pints	1 l
1 ton	1 t

1 gallon = 8 pints, which is approximately $(8 \div 1.75)$ 4.57 litres

16 ounces (oz) = 1 lb, so 8 oz is approximately $\frac{1}{4}$ kg or 250 g.

QUESTION:

A sign in France says that Paris is 48 km away. A bit later on another sign says that Paris is 23 km away. Approximately how many miles away is Paris on each occasion?

ANSWER:

When Paris is 48 km away

8 km	=	5 miles approximately
1 km	=	$\frac{5}{8}$ miles
48 km	=	$48 \times \frac{5}{8}$ miles
48 km	=	30 miles approximately

When Paris is 23 km away

8 km	=	5 miles approximately
1 km	=	$\frac{5}{8}$ miles
23 km	=	$23 \times \frac{5}{8}$ miles
23 km	=	14 miles approximately

QUESTION: Approximately how many pints are there in a 1.5 litre family-sized bottle of fizzy drink?

ANSWER:

1 l	=	1.75 pints approximately
1.5 l	=	1.5×1.75 pints

1.5 litres is approximately 2.5 pints

QUESTION:

Approximately how many ounces are there in $\frac{1}{2}$ kg of cheese?

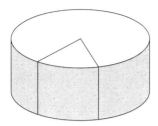

ANSWER:

1 lb = 16 oz

2 lb = 32 oz

1 kg = 2 lb approximately

1 kg = 32 oz

$\frac{1}{2}$ kg = $\frac{32}{2}$ oz

$\frac{1}{2}$ kg is approximately 16 oz

Perimeters

The perimeter of a shape is the total of the lengths of the sides of the shape. The perimeters of some simple shapes are shown in the diagrams.

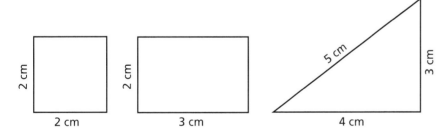

The perimeter of the square is 2 + 2 + 2 + 2 (or 4 × 2 cm) = 8 cm

The perimeter of the rectangle is 3 + 3 + 2 + 2 = 10 cm

The perimeter of the triangle is 3 + 4 + 5 = 12 cm

Areas by counting squares

Areas are measured in cm² (centimetre squared or sq. cm), m² or km², depending on the size of the area to be measured. The area of any 2-D shape can be worked out by counting squares on squared paper. Each square represents a cm², m² or km² depending on the units chosen.

The area of the square is 1 cm².

It is relatively easy to work out the area of a regular shape such as a square or rectangle.

For shapes that cover incomplete squares an approximate value for the area may be found by using the following method:

*   count the whole squares first
*   count the squares that are more than half covered
*   add these two counts together.

In the diagram the area of the rectangle is exactly 6 cm², the oval is approximately 12 cm², the triangle is approximately 10 cm², and the other shape is exactly 10 cm².

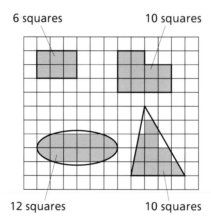

6 squares   10 squares

Each square = 1 cm²

12 squares   10 squares

Circumference of a circle

The circumference of a circle is another name for the perimeter of a circle. If you wrap a piece of string around the circumference of a circle, when you straighten the piece of string out and measure it, it gives you the perimeter of the circle.

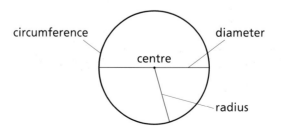

circumference

diameter

centre

radius

The relationship between of the circumference and diameter of a circle is given the special name of pi (a letter of the Greek alphabet), which has the symbol π.

$$\pi = \frac{\text{circumference}}{\text{diameter}}$$

No matter what size of circle is drawn, the value of π never changes; the circumference of a circle divided by its diameter always equals π. The actual value of π is not exact. The number of decimal places of π goes on forever. A value of 3.142 or 3 is often used as an approximate value for π.

Capacity by counting cubes

The volume of a 3-D shape can be worked out by counting the cubes in the shape. You cannot see all the cubes in a 3-D shape, so you have to 'visualise' the cubes. Think of the object being 'sliced up' into cubes. To work out the volume of a shape count the number of cubes on the side of the shape you can see, and multiply this number by the number of slices. The volume of a shape is measured in cm³ (centimetres cubed).

Each of the cubes in the examples is 1 cm³.

Number of cubes on front face	Number of slices	Number of cubes	Volume
6	3	6 × 3 = 18	18 cm³
12	2	12 × 2 = 24	24 cm³
24	3	24 × 3 = 72	72 cm³

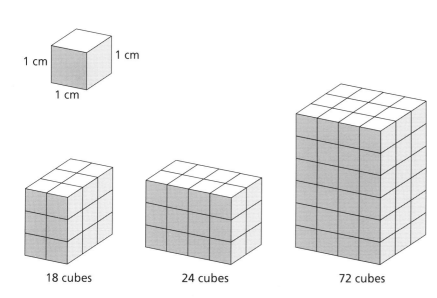

18 cubes   24 cubes   72 cubes

The circle

π is the ratio of the circumference of a circle to its diameter. It is not possible to write down the exact value of π because the decimal places for π go on forever. 3.142 is usually used as an approximate value for π. Sometimes, if an estimation is required, it is easier to use a value of 3 for π.

If:

C = circumference
d = diameter
r = radius

you can write the relationships between these variables as formulae.

$$\pi = \frac{circumference}{diameter} = \frac{C}{d}$$

The diameter is twice the radius, so

$d = 2r$

So $C = \pi d = 2\pi r$

The area (A) of a circle is given as:

$A = \pi r^2$

or $A = \pi \times \left(\frac{d}{2}\right)^2 = \frac{1}{4}\pi d^2$

QUESTION: Taking π as 3, work out the approximate circumferences and areas of the following circles.

d = 18 cm 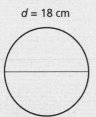   r = 12 cm 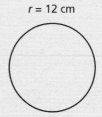   d = 15 cm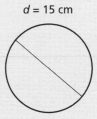

ANSWER:

Using $C = 2\pi r = \pi d$

The circumference of the first (left) circle is $C = 3 \times 18 = 54$ cm

The circumference of the second (middle) circle is $C = 2 \times 3 \times 12 = 72$ cm

The circumference of the third (right) circle is $C = 3 \times 15 = 45$ cm

Using $A = \pi r^2 = \frac{1}{4}\pi d^2$

The area of the first circle is $A = 0.25 \times 3 \times 18 \times 18 = 243$ cm^2

The area of the second circle is $A = 3 \times 12 \times 12 = 3 \times 144 = 432$ cm^2

The area of the third circle is $A = 0.25 \times 3 \times 15 \times 15 = 168.75$ cm^2

Areas of figures by formula

Working out the areas of shapes by counting squares is time-consuming. For some figures the area can be worked out using formulae. The formulae for calculating the areas of some common 2-D shapes are given in the diagrams and the table.

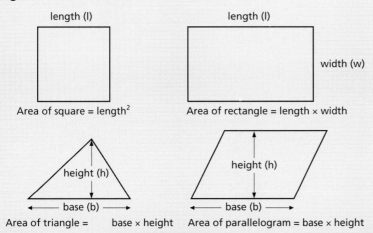

Area of square = length²   Area of rectangle = length × width

Area of triangle =   base × height   Area of parallelogram = base × height

Shape	Area (A)
Square	$A = l^2$
Rectangle	$A = lw$
Triangle	$A = \frac{1}{2}bh$
Parallelogram	$A = bh$

QUESTION: Find the area of each shape.

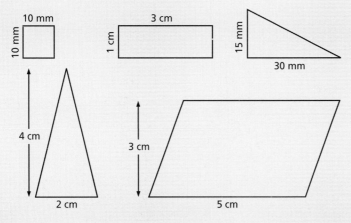

ANSWER:

The area of the square is $10 \times 10 = 100$ mm²

The area of the rectangle is $1 \times 3 = 3$ cm²

The area of the right-angled triangle is $0.5 \times 30 \times 15 = 225$ mm²

The area of the isosceles triangle is $0.5 \times 2 \times 4 = 4$ cm²

The area of the parallelogram is $5 \times 3 = 15$ cm²

Volumes of cuboids by formula

Three common cuboids are shown.
For each shape the formula for the volume is shown.

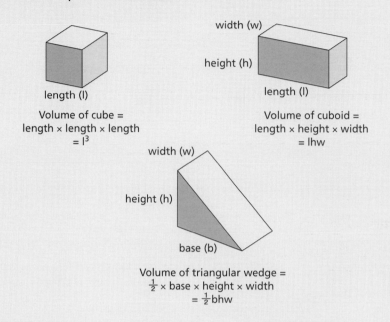

Volume of cube =
length × length × length
= l^3

Volume of cuboid =
length × height × width
= lhw

Volume of triangular wedge =
$\frac{1}{2}$ × base × height × width
= $\frac{1}{2}$bhw

QUESTION: Calculate the volume of each shape shown below.

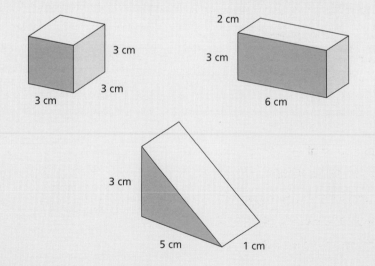

ANSWER:

The volume of the cube is $3 \times 3 \times 3 = 27$ cm³

The volume of the rectangular block is $6 \times 3 \times 2 = 36$ cm³

The volume of the triangular wedge is $0.5 \times 5 \times 3 \times 1 = 7.5$ cm³

CHAPTER 8

Collecting data

Data in everyday life

The examples show some of the different ways in which data are collected and presented in everyday life.

QUESTIONS: Using the sweet shop menu below

Item	Price
Choc bar	35p
Lemon fizzies	20p
Crisps	25p
Drink	50p
Ice cream	60p

a) How much would it cost to buy a choc bar and a drink?

b) What is the most expensive item in the shop?

c) What is the cheapest item in the shop?

d) How much would four packets of crisps cost?

e) Would it be cheaper to buy two lemon fizzies and one drink or one choc bar and one ice cream?

ANSWERS:

a) A choc bar and drink costs 35p + 50p = 85p.

b) The most expensive item in the shop is ice cream, priced at 60p.

c) The cheapest item in the shop is a lemon fizzy, priced at 20p.

d) Four packets of crisps cost 4 × 25p = £1.00.

e) Two lemon fizzies cost 2 × 20p = 40p.

One drink costs 50p, so two lemon fizzies and one drink cost 40p + 50p = 90p.

One choc bar and one ice cream cost 35p + 60p = 95p.

So it is cheaper to buy two lemon fizzies and one drink.

QUESTIONS: Using the menu below

Item	Small	Medium	Large
Plain burger	0.80	1.00	1.30
Cheeseburger	0.90	1.10	1.40
Doubleburger	1.40	1.75	1.90
Fries	0.70	0.90	1.20
Lemonade	1.00	1.20	1.50
Orange drink	1.00	1.20	1.50
Ice cream	1.00	1.50	1.80

Special: Medium plain burger, large fries, large drink £3.20

a) How much would it cost to buy a medium doubleburger, a medium orange drink and large fries?

b) Is it cheaper to buy a small doubleburger, small drink and small fries or a large plain burger, medium drink and medium fries?

c) If the items in the 'Special' were bought individually, how much more would it cost?

ANSWERS:

a) A medium doubleburger, a medium orange drink and large fries cost:
£1.75 + £1.20 + £1.20 = £4.15.

b) A small doubleburger, small drink and small fries cost:
£1.40 + £1.00 + £0.70 = £3.10
A large plain burger, medium drink and medium fries cost:
£1.30 + £1.20 + £0.90 = £3.40
So it is cheaper to buy a small doubleburger, small drink and small fries.

c) The individual items in a 'Special' are a medium plain burger, large fries and a large drink. Usually this costs:
£1.00 + £1.20 + £1.50 = £3.70.
A 'Special' costs £3.20 so there is a 50p saving in buying the 'Special'.

QUESTIONS: The table below is part of a train timetable for trains running between Wendon and Tenchester.

Monday to Saturday		Sunday	
Wendon	Tenchester	Wendon	Tenchester
Depart	Arrive	Depart	Arrive
06.00	08.30	07.00	10.00
07.00	09.30	08.00	11.00
08.00	10.30	09.00	12.00
09.00	11.45		
10.00	12.50		

a) Which train from Wendon should arrive in Tenchester at 11.00 on a Sunday?

b) How long should the journey take?

c) If you have to arrive at Tenchester before 10.00 each day between Monday and Friday, what train would you have to catch from Wendon?

d) How much longer is the train journey on Sundays compared to Monday to Saturday for the 07.00 train from Wendon?

ANSWERS:

a) 08.00 from Wendon

b) 3 hours

c) 07.00

d) 30 minutes

QUESTIONS: The table shows the results of an inter-school sports league.

Team	Played	Won	Drawn	Lost	Points
St Mary's	6	4	0	2	12
Holy Cross	4	4	0	0	12
Lawnfields	5	2	1	2	7
Park West	5	1	0	4	3

a) Which team has lost the most games?

b) Which teams have won more games than they have lost?

c) Which team has scored 7 points?

d) Explain why Holy Cross appears to be the best team so far.

ANSWERS:

a) Park West

b) St Mary's and Holy Cross

c) Lawnfields

d) Holy Cross and St Mary's have equal points of 12 but Holy Cross have not lost a game yet, and they have played two less games than St Mary's.

QUESTIONS: Part of a computer spreadsheet is shown below.

Name	Class	Contact	Tel. No.	Relationship
Mary Jones	4	Mr Jones	615423	Father
Sima Patel	4	Mrs Patel	246556	Mother
Tom Fraser	4	Mrs Pearce	989882	Neighbour
Chris Bartheuz	5	Mrs Bartheuz	233909	Mother
Tusia Clark	5	Mrs Clark	767676	Mother

a) Which child would be collected by a neighbour if he or she was sick?

b) Which class would Mr Jones go to to pick up Mary Jones?

c) How many children would have one of their parents pick them up?

ANSWERS:

a) Tom Fraser

b) Class 4

c) Four

Frequency tables

Frequency tables are used to record the number of times an event has occurred. For example, a football team wants to record the number of goals scored in each game they play. A 'tally' line is used to mark every time they score a goal in a game. After a period of time, the tally marks can be added together. This tells the team how frequently they score a certain number of goals in a game.

Number of goals scored in game	Tally	Frequency
0	III	3
1	IIIIII	6
2	IIII	4
3	II	2
4	IIII	4
5	II	2

Grouped data and class intervals

Instead of placing a tally against each number, it is sometimes better to group data into class intervals. A class interval is the width of each group.

QUESTION:
Heidi decided to do a survey of journey times to school for all the children in her class. The times were recorded in minutes. Using a class interval of 10 minutes, draw a frequency table from the data.

7	12	10	39
15	26	38	25
9	13	18	31
6	21	22	1
27	29	33	18

ANSWER:
Write down the class intervals, and count the number of times a number within each interval occurs. For example, there are four numbers that occur between 0 and 9. These are 7, 9, 6 and 1.
A tally mark for each of the four numbers is put against this class interval.

Class interval	Frequency
0–9	IIII
10–19	IIIIII
20–29	IIIIII
30–39	IIII

CHAPTER 9

Representing data

This chapter looks at different ways of displaying data.

Block (bar) charts

Block (bar) charts represent data with rectangular blocks.
The height of each block represents the frequency of the data.

QUESTION: The number of children whose birthdays fall on a
particular day of the week are shown in the table. Display this
information as a block chart.

Sun	Mon	Tues	Wed	Thur	Fri	Sat
9	7	10	5	12	7	8

ANSWER:

Number of children

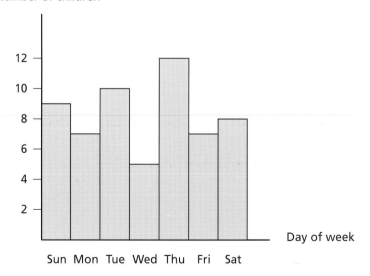

QUESTIONS: A class of children were asked what their favourite colour is. The results have been displayed as a bar chart.
Each square represents a child who likes the colour.

Number of children

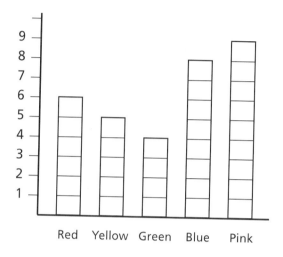

a) Which colour is the most popular?
b) Which colour is the least popular?
c) How many children like pink best?
d) How many children are there in the class?
e) How many children do not like red or pink the best?

ANSWERS:

a) Pink is the most popular colour because 9 children prefer it.
b) The least popular colour is green because only 4 children like it.
c) 9 children like pink the best.
d) There are 32 children in the class because there are 32 squares in total.
e) 15 children like red or pink the best, so 17 (32–15) children do not like red or pink the best.

QUESTION: The table shows how a child spends her £30 a month pocket money.

Item	Amount £	Symbol
Sweets	15.00	Sw
Magazines	5.00	M
Drinks	5.00	D
Toys	3.00	T
Savings	2.00	S

Represent the data on a bar graph.

ANSWER:

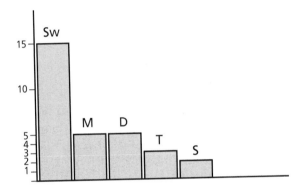

Pictograms

A pictogram uses symbols to represent groups of units. For example, a £1 coin can be used as the unit of money for the example of how pocket money is spent.

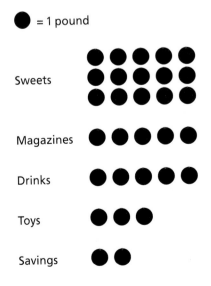

QUESTIONS: This graph shows the number of cars that passed the school gates between 8 am and 9 am during a school week.

Monday	
Tuesday	
Wednesday	
Thursday	
Friday	

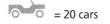 = 20 cars

= less than 20 cars

a) How many cars passed the school gates on Tuesday?

b) What was the least busy day?

c) What was the busiest day?

d) On which day did between 40 and 60 cars pass by?

ANSWERS:

a) 100 cars passed the school gates on Tuesday.

b) Monday was the least busy day (less than 60 cars).

c) The busiest day was Thursday (120 cars).

d) Between 40 and 60 cars passed by on Monday.

Vertical line graphs

Another way of representing data is to use vertical line graphs. Each line represents the frequency of the event.

QUESTION: A die is thrown repeatedly and the results are recorded in a table. Draw a vertical line graph to represent the frequencies of each score.

Score	1	2	3	4	5	6
Frequency	7	5	10	12	8	9

ANSWER:

Frequency

Line graphs

Line graphs are graphs in which a series of measurements are taken and plotted on paper, and a line is drawn through the points to connect each point. Line graphs are used to join up points that have been recorded in order to show a trend.

QUESTION: A child takes a maths test every week for 6 weeks. For each test the score is recorded in a table. Represent the data on a line graph and work out whether the child is getting better or worse at maths.

Test score	45	60	65	75	75	90
Week number	1	2	3	4	5	6

ANSWER:

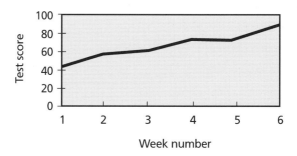

By looking at this graph you can see that there is an increase in test score. The test score has been steadily rising during the 6 week period. The child appears to be getting better at maths.

Pie charts

Pie charts are a useful way of displaying data when you have to show relative amounts.

QUESTION: The table shows how a child spends her £30 a month pocket money. Represent the data on a pie chart.

Item	Amount £
Sweets	15.00
Magazines	5.00
Drinks	5.00
Toys	3.00
Savings	2.00

ANSWER:

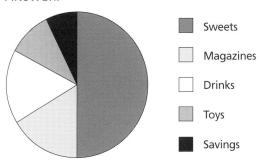

☐ Sweets

☐ Magazines

☐ Drinks

☐ Toys

☐ Savings

Making pie charts

The basis for drawing pie charts is the fact that there are 360° in a circle.

QUESTION: The table shows how Alicia spent her school day of 6 hours. Draw a pie chart to represent the data.

Subject	Hours
Maths	2
English	1
Sports	1
Science	2

ANSWER:
Divide 360° by 6, which gives the number of degrees to represent one hour. 360 ÷ 6 = 60°

Subject	Hours	Angle
Maths	2	2 × 60 = 120°
English	1	1 × 60 = 60°
Sports	1	1 × 60 = 60°
Science	2	2 × 60 = 120°

Using a protractor you can now draw the pie chart.

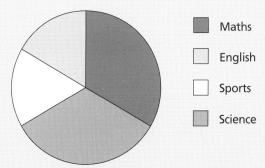

☐ Maths

☐ English

☐ Sports

☐ Science

Class intervals for continuous data

Discrete data are data that can be counted in convenient groups, for example the number of times a six is thrown on a die. You know that the number 6 is there. However, when something is measured the data are called continuous data, for example the height of children in a class. You do not know exactly what the height of any child might be. So continuous data are put into class intervals so that the results can be displayed.

QUESTION: A teacher keeps a record of how many minutes late children turn up to school. She divides the minutes into class intervals.

Minutes late	0–4	5–9	10–14	15–19
Number of children	9	7	4	2

Represent the data on a frequency diagram.

ANSWER:

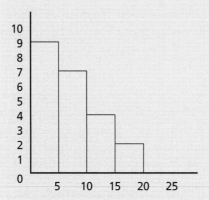

Scatter diagrams

Sometimes it is important to display two variables at the same time on the same graph, to look at whether there is any relationship between them. For example, if a child does a maths test, a science test and an English test, the child might want to see if there are any similarities in the results. For example, if the child is good at maths does this mean the child will also be good at science?

When the points are plotted on the same graph then the points will be scattered about. If there is a pattern or trend between the two variables then there is correlation between the two variables.

If one variable increases as the other variable increases, the correlation is positive. For example, there is a positive correlation between the amount of money someone earns and the amount of money that person spends.

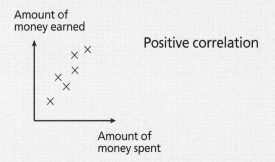

If one variable increases as the other variable decreases, the correlation is negative. For example, there is a negative correlation between the amount of money spent on heating and the temperature outside.

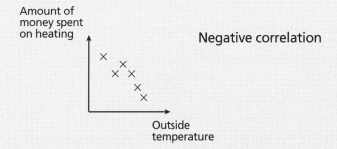

If the points are scattered and there is no trend or pattern then there is no correlation. For example, there is no correlation between the height of a child and the exam marks the child gets in a test.

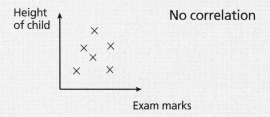

The examples shown above may seem obvious. However, there are times when the relationship between two variables is not so obvious. A scatter graph can be used to see if there is a relationship.

QUESTION: Given the test scores for a set of children, is there any evidence to suggest that those children who are good at maths are also good at science?

Name	Alicia	Mary	Lee	Sima	Rory	Cathy	Sunita	Nimish
Maths score	90	75	45	85	75	92	65	74
Science score	85	85	50	79	79	85	56	76

ANSWER: Plot each mark for each child on a graph. For example, Alicia scored 90 in the maths test and 85 in the science test, so plot this as a co-ordinate (90,85) on the graph. Repeat this for each child.
The name for each child is not shown on the graph because we are interested in the pattern or scatter of marks.

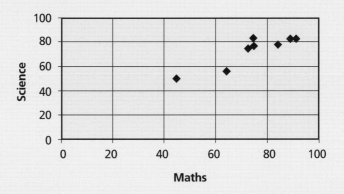

By looking at the graph there seems to be a positive correlation. Those children who scored well in maths also tended to score well in science.

QUESTION: For the same set of children, work out whether there is any relationship between children who score well in maths tests and height.

Name	Alicia	Mary	Lee	Sima	Rory	Cathy	Sunita	Nimish
Maths score	90	75	45	85	75	92	65	74
Height	132	152	140	133	127	129	143	140

ANSWER: Plot the scores as points on a graph.

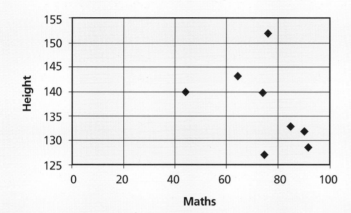

By looking at the graph there does not seem to be any relationship between maths score and height.

QUESTION: For the same set of children work out whether there is any relationship between the scores in maths and French tests.

Name	Alicia	Mary	Lee	Sima	Rory	Cathy	Sunita	Nimish
Maths score	90	75	45	85	75	92	65	74
French score	68	67	95	56	79	75	87	80

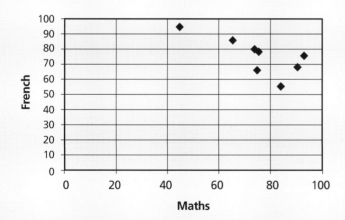

ANSWER: By looking at the graph there appears to be a negative correlation. This suggests that in this set of children, those children who scored well in the maths test scored less well in the French test, and those children who scored well in the French test scored less well in the maths test.

CHAPTER 10

Interpreting data

After mathematical data have been collected and displayed, the results often have to be analysed or interpreted.

Range

The range of a set of data is the difference between the highest value and the lowest value in the data set. The range is an estimate of the spread of data.

QUESTION: The lengths of 10 pencils in a pencil case are measured in centimetres. What is the range for the measurements recorded?
12.4, 12.2, 12.3, 12.3, 12.5

ANSWER: The length of each pencil varies between the lowest at 12.2 cm to the highest at 12.5 cm. The range is 12.5 – 12.2 = 0.3 cm.

The mean average

An average tells us the 'middle' value. The mean average is usually just called 'the average'. The example shows the method for calculating the mean average.

QUESTION: There are six children in a chess team with the following ages: 8, 9, 10, 10, 11, 12
Work out the range and average age of the team.

ANSWER: The range is worked out by subtracting the lowest value from the highest value in the set of data.

So the range is 12 – 8 = 4 years.

To work out the mean average, add up the ages of each child and divide the total of the ages by the total number of children in the team.

$$\text{The average (mean)} = \frac{8 + 9 + 10 + 10 + 11 + 12}{6}$$

$$= \frac{60}{6} = 10 \text{ years}$$

QUESTION: Work out the range and average pocket money for this group of children.

Name	Amount (£)
Joseph	3.00
Zak	5.50
Michael	4.00
Alicia	6.50
Mary	4.00

ANSWER:

Range = 6.50 – 3.00 = 3.50

Average (mean) = $\dfrac{3.00 + 5.50 + 4.00 + 6.50 + 4.00}{5}$ = $\dfrac{23}{5}$ = £4.60 pounds

QUESTION: Which team has the best goal-scoring average?

Team	Games played	Goals scored
Lechester Utd	10	14
Romney City	9	15
Whitington Town	11	16

ANSWER:

A team's goal-scoring average can be worked out by

$$\frac{\text{number of goals scored}}{\text{number of games played}}$$

Lechester Utd's goal-scoring average is $\frac{14}{10}$ = 1.40

Romney City's goal-scoring average is $\frac{15}{9}$ = 1.67

Whitington Town's goal-scoring average is $\frac{16}{11}$ = 1.45

So Romney City has the best goal-scoring average of 1.67 goals per game. Obviously it is not possible to score a fraction of a goal, but the average still provides an estimate of the number of goals scored.

QUESTION: The bar chart shows the number of lottery tickets sold each weekday. Draw a line on the graph to show the average (mean) number of lottery tickets sold in a week at a shop.

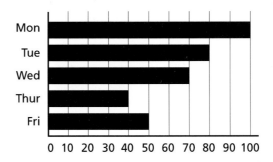

ANSWER:

Add up all the tickets sold for each day and divide by the number of days.

$$\frac{100 + 80 + 70 + 40 + 50}{5} = \frac{340}{5} = 68$$

Draw a vertical line at the point of 68 on the horizontal axis.

Modal average

Another type of average is called the modal average. The modal average is the most frequently occurring value in the data set.

QUESTION: A survey was conducted on the amount of pocket money each child received in a class. What is the modal average for the amount of pocket money received?

Name	Amount (£)	Name	Amount (£)
Sunita	3.00	Mark	4.00
Nimish	3.00	Lee	4.00
David	4.00	Alicia	6.50
Emily	5.50	Sima	4.50
Susan	4.50		

ANSWER: The modal average, the most frequently occurring pocket money value, is £4.00 (which occurs three times).

Median average

Another type of average is the median. The median average is the middle value after sorting the values in a data set in ascending order. If there is an even number in the data set then take the two middle values and divide by 2.

QUESTION: A survey was conducted on the amount of pocket money each child received in a class. What is the median average for the amount of pocket money received?

Name	Amount (£)
Sunita	3.00
Nimish	3.00
David	4.00
Emily	5.50
Susan	4.50
Mark	4.00
Lee	4.00
Alicia	6.50
Sima	4.50

ANSWER: Rearrange the data in ascending order.

Name	Amount (£)
Sunita	3.00
Nimish	3.00
David	4.00
Mark	4.00
Lee	**4.00**
Sima	4.50
Susan	4.50
Emily	5.50
Alicia	6.50

The median average is the middle value, so the median average is £4.00.

Misleading statistics

We know that the range is the difference between the highest and lowest values in a set of data. The range indicates the spread of data. This spread tells us whether the average we have used is a meaningful description of the sample.

For example, a survey is conducted of salaries in a local company and the salary of the managing director (owner) is included.

Employee	Amount (£)
Mr Jones (Managing Director)	120,000
Ms Patel	14,000
Mr White	20,500
Mr Andrews	17,000
Ms Brown	17,250
Mr Ceesay	15,500
Ms Ackling	21,000
Mr Harfield	17,000
Mr Hoskins	18,000

The average (mean) is worked out by adding each salary and dividing by the amount of employees, including the managing director.

120,000 + 14,000 + 20,500 + 17,000 + 17,250 + 15,500 + 21,000 + 17,000 + 18,000 = 260,250

Divide this total by the number of employees, 9. $\frac{260250}{9}$ = £28,916.67

The average has been calculated as £28,916.67. However, apart from the managing director, who owns the company, no one in the company earns as much as this. So in this case the average (mean) is not a good estimate or average to use. In fact, by using this average it could be misleading, because the average salary should reflect the salary that most employees earn.

If the salaries are rearranged in ascending order and a different average, such as the median average, is used, we get a different result.

Employee	Amount (£)
Ms Patel	14,000
Mr Ceesay	15,500
Mr Andrews	17,000
Mr Harfield	17,000
Ms Brown	**17,250**
Mr Hoskins	18,000
Mr White	20,500
Ms Ackling	21,000
Mr Jones (Managing Director)	120,000

The median average is £17,250. This is a much better reflection of the employees' salaries.

CHAPTER 11
Probability

Events

The ability to estimate or judge whether something will happen is very important and has many applications in maths, science and everyday life. When something happens it is usually called an event. Probability is the study of how likely an event is to occur. This chapter examines simple events that can be easily measured, such as tossing coins, drawing cards from a pack of cards, throwing dice.

It is important to use the terms fair and unfair when talking about events. For example:

- A fair coin means that a coin has an equal chance of showing heads or tails when tossed.
- A fair die is a die that has an equal chance of showing a number between 1 and 6 when thrown.
- A fair pack of cards is a pack in which every card has an equal chance of being picked.

The probability of drawing a card from an incomplete pack of cards is an example of an unfair event. When a fair coin is tossed there is an equally likely outcome of 'heads' (the front of the coin) or 'tails' (the back of the coin).

Fair coin

Heads

Tails

A die is a six-sided cube with one of the numbers 1 to 6 on each face. (The plural of die is dice.)

A pack of cards contains 52 cards, with four suits (of 13 cards each) called hearts, clubs, spades and diamonds. Hearts and diamonds are red suits and clubs and spades are black suits.

Spinners are symmetric shapes that may be spun on a stick and are similar to a die except that the faces are not necessarily numbered 1 to 6. The numbers may be chosen for each face, for example a spinner may be numbered as shown:

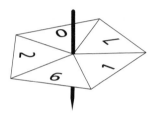

When an event occurs you need to work out whether the event is likely or not likely to occur. An event that is more likely to occur than not occur is called a 'probable' event. For example, the statement 'You will probably receive a birthday present from someone' means that there is a higher probability of receiving a birthday present than not receiving a birthday present.

If there is an equal chance of an event occurring, the event is said to be 'equally likely'.

Other names used for equally likely events are 'a 50-50 chance' and 'evens'.

Some events will definitely happen. These events are called certain events. An example of a certain event is 'The Sun will shine somewhere in the world tomorrow'.

An example of an event that is certain not to occur is 'You will grow three heads overnight'. This is an impossible event.

Probability scale

The probability of a certain event is given a value of 1. An impossible event is given a value of 0. Any other probability lies somewhere in the range between 0 and 1. The range of possible probabilities is often drawn on a probability scale.

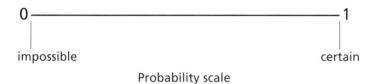

Probability scale

Weather reports often say that 'there is a 50-50 chance of rain tomorrow'. This means that there is a probability of $\frac{1}{2}$ that it will rain. A racehorse might be given odds of 'evens', which means the same as 50-50, so there is a probability of $\frac{1}{2}$ that the horse will win the race. If a coin is tossed then there are two possible outcomes, a head or a tail. There is a 1 in 2 chance of tossing a head and a 1 in 2 chance of tossing a tail. There is a probability of $\frac{1}{2}$ that the coin will land head-up, and a probability of $\frac{1}{2}$ that the coin will land tail-up. The probability of a half is shown on the probability scale.

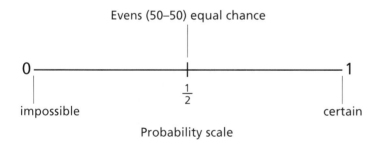

Probability scale

QUESTION: The following objects are dropped onto a hard floor. Estimate the probability of each object breaking and place each object at a suitable point on the probability scale.

Egg   Metal spoon   Plate   Thin glass   Toast

ANSWER:

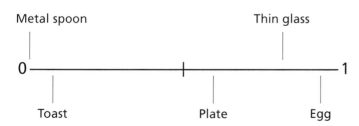

Estimating probability

Probability can be estimated by theoretical or experimental techniques. The probability of some events can be worked out if the objects have symmetry characteristics. If objects have symmetry characteristics, the outcomes are equally likely for each characteristic.

Object	Symmetry characteristics	Equally likely outcomes
Coin	2 equal sides. Equal chance of head or tail being tossed	Each side is equally likely to be tossed. There is a 1 in 2 chance of tossing a head and a 1 in 2 chance of tossing a tail.
Die	6 equal shaped sides. Equal chance of throwing a 1, 2, 3, 4, 5, or 6.	Each face is equally likely to be thrown. There is a 1 in 6 chance of throwing a 1, 2, 3, 4, 5 or 6.
Spinner	Equal shaped sides.	Each face has an equal chance of being landed on. Each face is equally likely to be spun.
Pack of cards	Each of the 52 cards look identical when they are face down.	Each card is assumed to be the same so that there is a 1 in 52 chance of picking any card. There is a 1 in 26 chance of picking a red card, and a 1 in 26 chance of picking a black card.

However, you may have to work out the outcome of an event occurring when there is not an equally likely outcome. Experiments can be used to estimate the probability of an event. For example, to work out the probability of the number of five-letter words on a page it is not possible to use symmetry because there are many different words all with different amounts of characters. One way to work out the probability would be to count the number of words with five letters and divide this number into the total number of words. By counting the words you have performed an experiment.

Other types of experiments may include counting the number of passengers travelling on a train journey or counting the number of telephone calls received at a company.

For experiments with computer models all the known facts are put into a computer program and an estimate of the outcome of an event occurring is calculated. An example of this is the weather forecast. Some of the most complex computer programs in the world are used to predict the weather. From these programs it is possible, for example, to estimate the probability of rain on a certain day.

Repeating experiments

Repeating the same experiment does not necessarily produce the same results. For example, if a coin is tossed 25 times then, using T for 'tails' and H for 'heads', the outcome may be as in the following table.

```
T   H   T   T   H
T   H   T   T   H
T   T   T   H   H
H   T   T   T   H
T   T   H   H   T
```

This experiment resulted in 15T and 10H.

If the experiment is repeated then the result may be something like 14H and 11T.

When experiments are performed using items with symmetric properties, we know the theoretical outcome. For example, the probability of tossing a coin and producing a head is one half. If a coin is tossed just a few times then it is unlikely that exactly half of the outcomes will be heads, and half tails. However, as the experiment is repeated many times the actual experimental results should become closer to the theoretical answer. For example, if a coin is tossed a 1000 times, it is likely that a head would be produced around 500 times, and a tail would be produced around 500 times.

Possible outcomes

If a coin is tossed once there are just two possible outcomes, H and T.

If two coins are tossed then there are four possible outcomes, but just three possible different outcomes. It does not matter whether the first coin shows a H and the second a T, or the first coin shows a T and the second a H as these two possible outcomes are equal.

QUESTION: Two coins are tossed. Write down the possible outcomes.

ANSWER:

```
H   T
H   H
T   T
T   H
```

QUESTION: Two coins are tossed. Write down the possible different outcomes.

ANSWER:

H   T

H   H

T   T

QUESTION: Three coins are tossed. Make a list of all the possible ways in which they could land. Make a list of all the different ways in which they could land.

ANSWER: A list of all possible outcomes is

T   T   H

T   T   T

T   H   H

H   T   T

T   H   T

H   T   H

H   H   T

H   H   H

A list of all possible different outcomes is

T   T   T

H   T   T

H   H   T

H   H   H

QUESTIONS: An ordinary pack of cards is shuffled and placed face down.

a) What is the probability of drawing a red card?

b) What is the probability of drawing a spade?

c) What is the probability of drawing the Jack of Hearts?

ANSWERS:

a) The probability of drawing a red card is $\frac{1}{2}$, as the card can be either red or black.

b) The probability of drawing a spade is $\frac{1}{4}$, as there are four suits and spades is just one suit.

c) The probability of drawing the Jack of Hearts is $\frac{1}{52}$ as the Jack of Hearts is just one card out of 52.

QUESTIONS: Two dice are thrown.

a) How many possible outcomes are there?

b) Which totals are least likely to occur?

c) Which totals are most likely to occur?

d) What is the probability of throwing a total of 8?

ANSWERS:

First draw a table.

+	1	2	3	4	5	6
1	2	3	4	5	6	7
2	3	4	5	6	7	8
3	4	5	6	7	8	9
4	5	6	7	8	9	10
5	6	7	8	9	10	11
6	7	8	9	10	11	12

a) All the possible outcomes are shown in the table.
   There are 36 possible outcomes.

b) There is only one way of throwing a 2 (1 and 1). There is only
   one way of throwing a 12 (6 and 6). The least likely totals are
   therefore 2 and 12. Both 2 and 12 have a 1 in 36 chance of
   being thrown.

c) The possible ways of throwing a 7 are (1 and 6), (2 and 5),
   (3 and 4), (4 and 3), (5 and 2) and (6 and 1).The most likely total
   is 7. There is a 6 in 36 or 1 in 6 chance of throwing a 7.

d) There are five possible ways of throwing an 8 (2 and 6), (3 and 5),
   (4 and 4), (5 and 3) and (6 and 2).The probability of throwing a
   total of 8 is therefore 5 in 36.

QUESTIONS: There are two spinners as shown.

a) Is there a 50-50 (evens) chance of spinning an even number on both spinners?

b) Are you more likely to spin a six on the six-sided spinner or on the eight-sided spinner?

c) Is it probable that a number higher than 6 is spun on the eight-sided spinner?

d) Are you less likely to spin a three on the six-sided spinner than on the eight-sided spinner?

e) Is it certain that you will spin a number between 2 and 5 on the six-sided spinner?

ANSWERS:

a) There is a 3 in 6 chance of spinning an even number on the six-sided spinner (2, 4 or 6), and there is a 4 in 8 chance of spinning an even number on the eight-sided spinner (2, 4, 6 or 8). So for both of these spinners there is an evens or 50-50 chance of spinning an even number.

b) There is a 1 in 6 chance of spinning a 6 on the six-sided spinner. There is a 1 in 8 chance of spinning a 6 on the eight-sided spinner. So it is more probable that a 6 is spun on the six-sided spinner.

c) There is only a 2 in 8 chance (or 1 in 4 chance) of spinning a number higher than 6 on the eight-sided spinner (7 and 8). There is therefore a 3 in 4 chance of not throwing a number higher than 6. So it is not probable that a number higher than 6 is spun on the eight-sided spinner.

d) There is a 1 in 6 chance of spinning a 3 on the six-sided spinner. There is a 1 in 8 chance of spinning a 3 on the eight-sided spinner. So it is not less likely that a 3 is spun on the six-sided spinner.

e) It is not certain that a number between 2 and 5 is spun on the six-sided spinner because the numbers 1 and 6 may be spun.

Probability as a fraction

If there are n equally likely events, then the probability (P) of one event occurring is $1/n$. You can write this as:

P(of event occurring in n equally likely events) $= \dfrac{1}{n}$

Example: The probability of tossing a head on a coin can be written as

P(head) $= \dfrac{1}{2}$

Example: The probability of rolling a three on a die can be written as

P(rolling a three) $= \dfrac{1}{6}$

Example: The probability of rolling an even number on a die can be written as

P(rolling an even number) $= \dfrac{3}{6} = \dfrac{1}{2}$

Example: The probability of choosing a red card from a pack of cards can be written as

P(red card) $= \dfrac{26}{52} = \dfrac{1}{2}$

Example: The probability of drawing a club from a pack of cards can be written as

P(club) $= \dfrac{13}{52} = \dfrac{1}{4}$

QUESTIONS: There are 18 coloured marbles in a bag.
There are 3 red marbles, 12 blue marbles and 3 green marbles.

a) What is the probability of picking a blue marble?

b) What is the probability of picking a red marble?

c) What is the probability of picking a red or blue marble?

d) Is there a higher probability of picking a blue marble rather than a red or green marble?

ANSWERS:

a) P(picking a blue marble) $= \dfrac{12}{18} = \dfrac{2}{3}$

b) P(red marble) $= \dfrac{3}{18} = \dfrac{1}{6}$

c) P(red or blue marble) $= \dfrac{15}{18} = \dfrac{5}{6}$

d) $P(\text{blue}) = \frac{2}{3}$ is approximately 0.67

$P(\text{red or green}) = \frac{6}{18} = \frac{1}{3}$ is approximately 0.33

As 0.67 > 0.33 then there is a higher probability of picking a blue marble.

Independent events

If two events occur at the same time and the two events do not affect each other, then these events are said to be independent events. For example, if two coins are tossed the possible outcome of one coin is totally independent of the second coin. If two dice are thrown, the possible outcome of the first die is totally independent of the possible outcome of the second die.

Two events A and B are independent if the probability of both A and B occurring is equal to the probability of A occurring multiplied by the probability of B occurring. This can be written as:

$P(\text{A and B}) = P(\text{A}).P(\text{B})$

QUESTION: Two coins are tossed. What is the probability of tossing two heads?

ANSWER:

For the first coin, $P(\text{H}) = \frac{1}{2}$

For the second coin, $P(\text{H}) = \frac{1}{2}$

The probability of tossing two heads is:

$P(\text{H and H}) = \frac{1}{2} \times \frac{1}{2} = \frac{1}{4}$

It is possible to check this result by considering the possible outcomes. If two coins are tossed there are four possible outcomes:

H H
H T
T T
T H

There is only one chance of tossing two heads out of the four different outcomes. So the probability is $\frac{1}{4}$.

QUESTION: What is the probability of tossing a head on a coin and drawing an ace from a pack of cards?

ANSWER:

As these two events are independent

$P(H \text{ and Ace}) = P(H).P(\text{Ace})$

$P(H) \quad = \frac{1}{2}$

$P(\text{Ace}) = \frac{4}{52} = \frac{1}{13}$

$P(H \text{ and Ace}) = \frac{1}{2} \times \frac{1}{13} = \frac{1}{26}$

Sum of probabilities

The sum of the probabilities of all possible outcomes following an event is equal to 1.

Example: Consider tossing a coin.

$P(H) = \frac{1}{2}, P(T) = \frac{1}{2}$

The probability of tossing a H or a T can be written as:

$P(H) + P(T) = \frac{1}{2} + \frac{1}{2} = 1$

Example: Consider throwing a die.

$P(1) = \frac{1}{6}$

$P(2) = \frac{1}{6}$

$P(3) = \frac{1}{6}$

$P(4) = \frac{1}{6}$

$P(5) = \frac{1}{6}$

$P(6) = \frac{1}{6}$

The probability of throwing a 1, or 2, or 3, or 4, or 5, or 6 can be written as:

$$P(1) + P(2) + P(3) + P(4) + P(5) + P(6) = 1$$

Example: Consider drawing a card from a pack of cards.

$P(\text{red card}) = \dfrac{1}{2}$

$P(\text{black card}) = \dfrac{1}{2}$

The probability of drawing a red card or black card can be written as:

$$P(\text{red card}) + P(\text{black card}) = 1$$

QUESTION: There are some blue balls, green balls and yellow balls in a box. If the probability of picking a blue ball is equal to the probability of picking a yellow ball and the probability of picking a green ball is $\dfrac{1}{4}$, calculate the probability of picking a blue ball.

ANSWER:

We know

$P(\text{blue}) = P(\text{yellow})$ and

$P(\text{green}) = \dfrac{1}{4}$

We know that the probability of picking a green ball and a blue ball and a yellow ball is 1.

$$P(\text{green}) + P(\text{blue}) + P(\text{yellow}) = 1$$

Using $P(\text{green}) = \dfrac{1}{4}$

$P(\text{blue}) + P(\text{yellow}) = 1 - P(\text{green})$

$1 - \dfrac{1}{4} = \dfrac{3}{4}$

$P(\text{blue}) = P(\text{yellow})$

So $2 \times P(\text{blue}) = \dfrac{3}{4}$

Therefore $P(\text{blue}) = \dfrac{3}{8}$

Probability of an event not occurring

Events will either occur or not occur. Because the total of all possibilities following an event is 1, it is possible to work out the probability of an event not occurring. This can be written as:

probability of the event occurring + probability of the event not occurring = 1, or

P(event occurring) + P(event not occurring) = 1.

Example: If the probability of an event occurring is $\frac{1}{4}$ then it is possible to calculate the probability of an event not occurring:

$\frac{1}{4}$ + P(event not occurring) = 1

So P(event not occurring) = $1 - \frac{1}{4} = \frac{3}{4}$.

QUESTION: There is a 1 in 4 chance of the Sun shining in London tomorrow. Calculate the probability of the Sun not shining in London tomorrow.

ANSWER:

P(Sunshine in London tomorrow) = $\frac{1}{4}$

P(No sunshine in London tomorrow) = $1 - \frac{1}{4} = \frac{3}{4}$.